Must Come Assembled

Must Come Assembled

The Strength Beyond Me
Living by God's Power When Mine Runs Out

Dr. John F. Groves Sr.

Must Come Assembled

Copyright © 2026 by Dr. John F. Groves

ISBN: 978-1-971712-16-1

Quill and Company Publishing

QuillandCompany.com
TheQuillandCompany@gmail.com

Dedication

This book is dedicated to you.

To you—the man who has poured out everything you had in your relationships, often without receiving enough in return to refill what was emptied. You've given your strength, your patience, your love, and your presence, even on the days when you felt hollow inside. You've carried responsibilities that others never saw, and you kept moving forward because people were counting on you, even when you had nothing left to give.

You know what it feels like to push through exhaustion.

To lead when you feel lost.

To love when you feel unseen.

To keep going when your tank is on empty and there is no light showing you the way.

I wrote this book because of you—and for you.

Because I understand the weight you've been carrying.

Because I've lived in that same quiet struggle.

Because I know how heavy it feels to be strong for everyone else while silently wondering who will be strong for you.

So hear me clearly: you are seen. You are heard. You are appreciated.

Your effort matters.

Your heart matters.

Your sacrifices matter.

And your pain is not a sign of weakness—it is evidence of how deeply you've loved and how faithfully you've shown up.

As you turn these pages, my hope is that you find something you may not have felt in a long time: restoration.

That you rediscover your worth.

That you remember you deserve to be poured into, supported, and understood.

That you realize you were never meant to carry everything alone.

This book is for you—the man who whispered "I'm tired" and kept going anyway.

May you find strength here.

May you find clarity here.

May you find yourself here.

Foreword

Over the last decade or so I have spent time talking to men—soldiers and CEOs, young fathers and aging widowers, men with calloused hands and men with calloused hearts. I have sat across from them in hospital rooms, coffee shops, boardrooms, and back pews. And if there is one truth I have learned about men, it is this:

Most of them are carrying far more than anyone knows.

They carry the weight of families they love, jobs that demand, wounds they never named, expectations they inherited, and fears they never confessed. They carry responsibility like oxygen—quietly, constantly, unquestioned. And they carry it long after their strength has begun to fray.

For years I watched good men crumble under the myth that they were supposed to be selfsustaining. I watched them pray last, rest rarely, and apologize for their limits as if God expected them to be made of steel instead of dust. I watched them confuse burnout with failure and exhaustion with shame. And I watched them hide—behind competence, behind humor, behind silence.

That is why this book matters.

It does not shame men for being tired. It does not flatter them for being strong. It tells the truth Scripture has been whispering since Eden:

Strength was never meant to begin with us.

What you hold in your hands is not another manual on grit, discipline, or spiritual performance. It is a gentle but unflinching invitation back to the Source. It is a reminder that the God who formed men from dust never expected them to live as if they were granite.

As I read these chapters, I found myself nodding, remembering faces—men I've counseled, prayed for, buried, and blessed. Men who tried to hold their worlds together with clenched fists until God, in mercy, taught them to open their hands. Men who discovered that dependence is not weakness but worship. Men who learned that the strongest thing a man can do is lean.

This book gives language to what many men have felt but never articulated. It exposes the lies that have exhausted them and replaces them with truths that can sustain them. It offers rhythms that work in real lives, not ideal ones. And it points every man—not to himself, not to his stamina, not to his résumé—but to the God who carries what no man was built to survive holding.

If you are reading this as a man who is tired, welcome. If you are reading this as a man who is faithful but stretched thin, welcome. If you are reading this as a man who has quietly whispered, "Lord, I can't do this anymore," you are exactly where God does His best work.

My prayer is simple: May these pages become a turning point. May they loosen what has been clenched too long. May they teach you to breathe again. May they lead you—not into a heavier version of masculinity, but into a holier one.

And when you reach the final chapter, I hope you can say what I have said for many years now:

"I am still standing—not because I was strong enough, but because God was faithful."

Preface

This book is written for men.

Not because strength belongs to men alone—but because men have been taught the wrong version of it for a long time.

Most men were never told they could depend on God without forfeiting their dignity. We were taught to carry weight quietly. To produce. To provide. To endure. To fix what breaks and absorb what hurts. Faith, somewhere along the way, became something we practiced *after* responsibility—not the strength that carried it.

So, we learned to pray last.
To ask for help late.
To call exhaustion discipline.
To call burnout duty.

And when our strength finally ran out, we didn't know what to do with the silence that followed.

I know this because I've lived it too.

Years ago, I found myself sitting in my car outside a hospital at 2 a.m., hands shaking on the steering wheel, whispering a prayer that sounded more like a confession: "God, I don't have anything left." I wasn't faithless. I wasn't rebellious. I was simply empty—and terrified that emptiness meant failure. What I discovered in that parking lot is what this book is written to tell you: emptiness is often the doorway where God finally fills.

This book is not written to make men feel better about being tired. It is written to tell the truth about why we are tired—and what God has been offering us all along.

Scripture never presents strength as something a man generates. It presents it as something a man receives. From the first breath God breathed into dust, strength has always been borrowed. Sustained. Given daily. Withdrawn when we insist on carrying life alone.

"I can do all things through Christ which strengtheneth me."
—Philippians 4:13 (KJV)

That verse is not a slogan.

It is a surrender.

Across these chapters, we will walk from self-reliance into surrender, from exhaustion into endurance, from pressure into presence.

This book will not flatter you. It will not shame you. It will not tell you to grind harder, pray louder, or fix yourself before God meets you. It will tell you—again and again—that you were never meant to be strong *by yourself.*

If you are a man who feels responsible for more than you can carry…
If you are faithful but worn…
If you lead others while quietly running on empty…
If your strength is thinning and your prayers are shorter than they used to be…

You are not disqualified.
You are not failing.
You are being invited.

This book is an invitation to unlearn the lie that dependence is weakness—and to rediscover the kind of strength that lasts.

Read slowly.
Read honestly.

And don't rush past the places that feel uncomfortable.
The places that feel uncomfortable are often the places God begins.

Contents

Introduction

There comes a moment in a man's life when strength stops responding to effort.

Nothing necessarily explodes. No single tragedy announces the shift. Responsibilities remain. Phones still buzz. Bills still wait. Life keeps moving. But somewhere beneath the surface, something folds. The inner voice that once said, *You can handle this*, grows quiet. Not because the load suddenly increased—but because personal strength has reached its ceiling.

Many men recognize that moment by its silence.

Effort no longer produces traction. Prayer feels like voicemail. Sleep no longer restores. You lie awake wondering how much longer a human frame can pretend to be titanium. It is an unsettling realization—not that life is hard, but that self-reliance has limits.

Our culture rewards the illusion of unlimited capacity. It salutes the man who never taps out, never lets on, never slips. Strength is measured by endurance without complaint. And inside church walls, the message can sound similar—believe more, serve more, lead more, dig deeper. The language changes, but the plot stays the same: *real men push through*. If they collapse, they must have pushed wrong.

That story is quietly grinding holes in men's souls.

Scripture tells a different one.

From Adam's first breath to Paul's prison-cell letters, holy strength has always been borrowed strength. God never asked men to power their own lives; He invited them to live connected to His. Strength was never meant to originate within human capacity. It was designed to flow from God, through men, and into the lives they were called to steward.

The trouble is, many men were never shown how to live that way without feeling emasculated, irresponsible, or unspiritual. Dependence was framed as weakness. Rest felt like retreat. Needing help felt like failure. So men learned to wait until the tank rattled on fumes before praying seriously—hoping for a quick spiritual refill before Monday morning.

It is a miserable system.
It leaves men ashamed of their limits and suspicious of grace.

This book will not offer techniques for superior stamina. It will not demand louder declarations, heavier lifts, or earlier alarm clocks. It will not promise that faith eliminates fatigue. Instead, it walks into the frighteningly honest place where men admit they were designed to need help every single day.

Here, dependence is not treated as a step backward. It is presented as the doorway into a strength that outlasts sleep cycles, market crashes, health scares, and mid-life detours. A strength that holds when effort no longer does.

Along the way, four stubborn myths will be confronted—myths that quietly exhaust good men:

- That a real man should be self-sufficient
- That burnout means faith was mismanaged
- That strong men don't get tired if they're spiritual enough
- That God's power is a backup plan instead of the main power line

Each myth will be brought into the light, tested against Scripture, and exchanged for a truth that frees both conscience and shoulders.

Beneath those themes runs one central truth: strength was never supposed to start with you. It was meant to come to you. That changes everything—how mornings begin, how decisions are made, how children are held, how teams are led, how devastating news is processed, and how sleep comes when nothing external has changed.

When the source shifts, the strain shifts.
Dependence stops being an emergency button and becomes the operating system.

Most men carry more than titles, tasks, or budgets. They carry the unspoken promise to be okay for everyone else. Expectations inherited from fathers who modeled stone-faced endurance. From mentors who never flinched. From churches that applauded reliability but rarely asked about weariness. Many carry memories they do not talk about—losses, failures, deployments, divorces, secrets. And underneath it all sits the fear that if one finger loosens its grip, everything will collapse and confirm what they've quietly worried all along.

This book exists to say clearly: you are not alone, and you are not broken.

What will you gain by turning these pages? First, permission—the holy kind—to stop confusing limitation with failure. You will gain language to read familiar verses with fresh eyesight.

Philippians 4:13 will shrink from bravado into confession.

John 15:5 will sound less like rebuke and more like oxygen.

You will learn rhythms of daily dependence that work in real lives with real schedules—practices that train the soul to lean, listen, and let God carry what would otherwise crush a man.

You will also gain language to offer other men. Language that works over coffee and in hospital corridors. Language that goes deeper than clichés and stronger than silence. Language that invites God into spaces long guarded by pride or fear.

Most of all, you will gain hope—not the kind that sparkles for a weekend and fades by Wednesday, but the kind anchored in a God who has never lost a man who leaned hard on Him. Hope that lifts when strength thins, holds when the future feels fragile, and whispers when words run out.

The God revealed in these pages does not shame men for being dust. He remembers that they were dust before they ever sinned. And He still breathes strength into dust today, just as surely as He did in Eden.

Read slowly.
Read honestly.
Notice the places that make you defensive—those are often pride wearing the mask of duty. Notice the places that sting—those are often scars God intends to heal. And beneath every chapter, listen for the steady invitation to trade the heavy myth of self-made strength for the lighter yoke Jesus promised.

If you have already whispered, *"Lord, I can't do this anymore,"* you are in the right place.
If you haven't yet, keep reading. The day will come.

This journey is not about becoming less of a man.
It is about becoming the kind of man God always had in mind—strong because he stays connected, steady because he knows where his help comes from, and free because he no longer has to pretend he is limitless.

Turn the page.
There is strength waiting beyond the edge of your own.

PART I — When Strength Runs Out

Chapter 1 - Built to Need God

Lie: Strong men shouldn't reach limits.

Truth: Most men do not fail because they are weak. They fail because they try to be strong alone.

Strength, as most men inherit it, is quiet. It does not announce itself or ask permission. It carries. It fixes. It absorbs pressure without comment. Long before masculinity is explained, it is observed—learned through moments rather than lessons. A man watches who lifts the heavy thing, who stays late, who solves the problem, who does not complain. Over time, strength becomes synonymous with usefulness, and usefulness becomes identity.

I remember watching grown men when I was young—how they moved through rooms without asking for help, how they tightened their jaw when something hurt, how they stepped in front of difficulty like it was expected of them. No one sat me down to teach this. You simply absorb it. You learn that the man who needs nothing is the man who can be counted on. You learn that silence is maturity, that selfcontainment is virtue, that asking for help is something you do only when the situation becomes embarrassing.

If you can lift it, you lift it. If you can repair it, you repair it. If it hurts, you keep that part quiet.

This version of strength feels responsible. It feels honorable. It often looks faithful. But it is incomplete.

Because Scripture never defines strength as selfsufficiency. It defines strength as alignment—being rightly positioned under the sustaining power of God. From the beginning, men were not designed to operate as independent systems. They were created dependent, sustained, and limited by design.

"Then the LORD God formed man of the dust of the ground, and breathed into his nostrils the breath of life; and man became a living soul." —Genesis 2:7 (KJV)

The image is deliberate. Man does not begin with motion, will, or capacity. He begins as dust—formed, shaped, and lifeless until God breathes. Life does not originate within the man; it enters him. Strength is not generated. It is received.

And this moment occurred before sin. Before shame. Before work became toil. Which means dependence is not a flaw introduced by the Fall—it is the original design. Humanity did not become needy because it was broken. Humanity was created needy because it was meant to live connected.

Men often interpret limits as evidence of failure. Scripture treats limits as coordinates. They point us toward the source of life rather than away from it. There has never been a version of you—past, present, or imagined—that could thrive without God. Capacity was always meant to be borrowed in real time, not stored for independent use.

Even in Eden, the rhythm was dependence.

Adam's first full day of existence was not work but rest—delighting in God's finished labor. Responsibility came after relationship. Effort followed grace. The order matters. God did not wait for man to exhaust himself before inviting rest; He built rest into the beginning.

Imagine that: the first sunrise Adam ever saw was not a call to productivity but an invitation to enjoy what God had already completed. Before

Adam ever tilled soil or named a creature, he learned that life begins with receiving, not performing. That rhythm has never changed. Yet many men live as though it has.

Life is organized around capacity. Calendars are filled. Responsibilities stack. Prayer becomes reactive rather than foundational. God is consulted when strength thins, not acknowledged as its source. Faith becomes supplemental—useful when pressure increases, unnecessary when things feel manageable.

Jesus addressed this directly.

"I am the vine, ye are the branches… for without me ye can do nothing." — John 15:5 (KJV)

Nothing is not exaggeration. It is not metaphorical softness. It is a statement of reality. A branch may retain its shape when separated from the vine, but it no longer carries life. Fruit does not come from effort; it comes from connection.

Most men do not wake up intending to live disconnected from God. They simply drift into selfreliance in small, respectable ways. They manage schedules efficiently. They solve problems quietly. They keep things moving. The fruit may even look impressive for a time. But Jesus reminds us that apart from Him, nothing of lasting value is produced. What appears strong may still be hollow.

Drift rarely announces itself. It feels like competence. It feels like maturity. It feels like "I've got this." A man wakes up, handles his responsibilities, checks the boxes, and never notices that he hasn't prayed in days—not because he's rebellious, but because he's capable. And capability, when left unchecked, becomes a counterfeit source.

Selfreliance is not always loud. Often it wears church clothes. It sings on pitch. It serves faithfully. It preaches discipline while quietly trusting productivity more than providence. It measures holiness by how little help a man requires and admires endurance that never pauses long enough to ask where the strength is coming from.

Scripture offers a different definition.

Strength is not portrayed as internal reserve but as overflow. It is what happens when a man abides so deeply in the presence of God that divine life saturates his limitations. Moses descends Sinai radiant. David stands before a giant unarmored. Elijah outruns a chariot. Fishermen speak languages they never studied.

None of these moments originate in superior willpower. They occur because ordinary men step into the current of God's ability. Their stories are not about exceptional men but about exceptional dependence. The pattern is consistent: God takes limited men, fills them with His presence, and produces outcomes no human discipline could manufacture.

Just as importantly, Scripture never hides the limits of these same men. David weeps in caves. Elijah collapses under a tree. Moses grows weary. Their weakness is not disqualifying—it is the canvas on which God displays His sufficiency.

This reframes masculinity entirely.

Strength is not the absence of need. It is the wisdom to know where need is met.

Receiving, however, runs against instinct. Lifting feels productive. Carrying feels admirable. Receiving requires posture—open hands, unguarded honesty, the admission that what you have is not enough. Jesus taught this posture plainly: Give us this day our daily bread. Not stored supply. Not future security. Daily dependence.

And daily dependence is uncomfortable. It means you cannot stockpile spiritual strength. It means you cannot live off yesterday's prayer life. It means you cannot treat God like a backup generator. It means you must return, again and again, to the One who gives breath.

God has never offered men a onetime charge. He offers connection.

This chapter is not a call to abandon responsibility. It is a call to stop carrying responsibility alone. Dependence is not the last resort of failing men; it is the starting line of faithful ones. Exhaustion is not proof that you are weak—it is often evidence that you have been trying to live disconnected from the source of strength.

You were built to need God. Limits were woven into your frame on purpose. Not to shame you—but to guide you.

As this book continues, we will explore what happens when strength runs out and how God meets men there. For now, settle into the truth that has been present since the first breath was drawn from dust: you were never meant to do this alone.

That is not weakness. That is design.

Chapter 2 - Burnout Isn't a Failure— It's a Signal

Lie: If I burn out, I've mismanaged my faith.

Truth: Burnout is often the result of carrying what God never assigned you to carry alone.

Burnout is rarely planned. It is almost always ignored.

It does not arrive with sirens or headlines. It begins as a warning light—small, dismissible, easy to rationalize because the engine is still running. Men quote Scripture, drink another cup of coffee, tighten their resolve, and keep moving. Responsibility demands it. Expectations reinforce it. Strength, as they understand it, requires endurance.

And because men are conditioned to push through discomfort, the early signs feel too minor to matter. A shorter temper. A shorter prayer. A longer stare at the ceiling at 2 a.m. Nothing dramatic enough to justify slowing down. Nothing obvious enough to call "burnout." Just a quiet erosion that feels like life.

Then one ordinary day, the dashboard goes dark.

Burnout is not collapse; it is silence. Something inside that used to respond no longer does. Emotion dulls. Prayer shortens. Sleep stops restoring. The man is still functioning, but the inner engine has seized. Not from laziness. Not from moral failure. From prolonged strain without replenishment.

Burnout is not a verdict. It is a signal.

Men often speak of burnout with embarrassment, as if naming it reveals a private deficiency. But burnout is not a character flaw—it is physics. Prolonged output without intake leads to depletion. Remove fuel and flame fades. Human bodies, emotions, and spirits operate under the same unyielding laws.

The shame enters when exhaustion is moralized.

Instead of asking, *What have I been running on?* Men ask, *What's wrong with me?*

Scripture never treats tiredness as rebellion. Jesus sleeps in a storm. Elijah collapses beneath a tree. Paul writes of being pressed beyond strength. None are rebuked. None apologize. Fatigue is treated as reality, not sin.

Burnout becomes dangerous only when misunderstood.

Selfreliance accelerates exhaustion because it works—temporarily. Men are rewarded for being dependable, capable, and quiet. They absorb more responsibility because they can. Each decision feels faithful in isolation. Together they create a pattern where strength quietly shifts from God to grit.

And grit is a terrible substitute for grace.

Like Samson shaking himself after his strength had left, men assume capacity will always be there because it always has been. Until one day it isn't.

That moment, as humiliating as it feels, is mercy.

Burnout is not God punishing effort. It is God interrupting a pattern that would eventually destroy the man He loves.

The signal is loud because whispering didn't work.

When burnout hits, one of the first necessities is separating conviction from condemnation. Conviction corrects behavior and points forward. Condemnation attacks identity and offers no path. Conviction says, *You are carrying weight outside My design.* Condemnation says, *You are weak and unworthy.*

Jesus invites the weary. Condemnation drives men to perform harder to prove value. The source of the voice matters.

Burnout is not always a sign you chose the wrong calling. It does not automatically mean you should quit everything. It is not proof that prayer failed or faith was deficient. Burnout asks for diagnosis before decisions.

If you listen carefully, burnout speaks in rhythms, not accusations:

- Pace has exceeded presence
- Responsibility has outgrown communion
- Schedule has crowded out Sabbath
- Fear has grown larger than prayer

Notice the language. These are alignment issues, not moral ones.

Men are often trained to respond only to catastrophic failure. Scripture invites earlier listening. Tension in the body, irritability at home, indifference toward prayer—these are not nuisances to suppress but signals to interpret. God gave you a nervous system as surely as He gave you a soul. Paying attention to either is stewardship.

And ignoring either is neglect.

Jesus models this rhythm. He pours Himself out, then withdraws. He refuses crowds to rest. He does not apologize for pacing Himself according to the Father. When the disciples return energized from ministry, He does not assign more work. He calls them away to rest before burnout ever begins.

Elijah's story makes the point unmistakable. After extraordinary faithfulness, he collapses and prays to die. God does not rebuke him. He feeds him. He lets him sleep. Only after physical restoration does spiritual revelation follow. The journey was too much—not because Elijah lacked faith, but because God designed humans to require replenishment.

Burnout exposes an illusion men rarely question: control.

Stopping feels irresponsible because it threatens the belief that everything depends on you. Burnout reveals that this was never true. Letting go does not cause collapse—it reveals who has been holding things together all along.

At the root of burnout is often proving. Men prove reliability, competence, faithfulness. Proving itself is not sin, but when proving replaces abiding, exhaustion is inevitable. Abiding produces fruit naturally. Proving manufactures outcomes through force.

Burnout feels like failure. In truth, it is often reorientation.

This chapter does not offer quick fixes. It offers clarity. Burnout is not the end of usefulness—it is an invitation to return to the Source of strength before usefulness becomes destruction.

In the next chapter, we will confront a related truth: even strong men still get tired. Weariness does not disappear once dependence is restored because humanity remains finite. But weariness, rightly understood, no longer carries shame.

For now, hear the signal without fear. It is not accusing you. It is guiding you home.

Chapter 3 — Strong People Still Get Tired

Lie: If I were stronger spiritually, I wouldn't be this exhausted.

Truth: Fatigue is not evidence of weak faith—it's evidence of human flesh.

There is a particular kind of panic that comes with being tired.

Not the normal tiredness of a long day—but the quieter fear that whispers, *A stronger man wouldn't feel this.* Exhaustion doesn't just drain energy; it accuses. It suggests you are failing the people you love and disappointing the God you serve. And because most men have been trained to equate strength with steadiness, fatigue feels like exposure.

It feels like someone has peeled back the exterior and revealed the truth you've been trying to outrun: *You are not limitless.*

Somewhere along the way, many of us merged stamina with holiness.

If our eyes sag, our prayers must be thin. If our body demands rest, our faith must be flimsy. If we can't keep going, we must be doing something wrong.

But Scripture never makes that connection.

Human limitation is assumed from the first page of the Bible. Holiness is something else entirely. Tiredness is not a verdict on your devotion. It is proof you are still made of dust.

That statement alone can free a man—if he lets it.

Fatigue often feels like failure because the world rewards the appearance of endless capacity. Even in church spaces, reliability is praised so consistently that weariness becomes embarrassing. Men learn to serve until they are empty and then apologize for the emptiness, as if they committed a moral offense by being finite.

Some men even hide their fatigue like a secret sin. They push through headaches, numbness, irritability, and spiritual dryness because slowing down feels like letting someone down. They don't want to disappoint their pastor, their wife, their children, or their own expectations of what a "strong man" should be.

But Scripture does not rebuke tired people. It meets them.

Consider Elijah.

Elijah was not weak. He had watched fire fall from heaven. He had outrun a chariot. He had confronted kings and toppled idol worship. If strength were measured by spiritual intensity, Elijah would qualify as elite. Yet one chapter later he is walking into the wilderness, praying to die.

"And he requested for himself that he might die; and said, It is enough; now, O LORD, take away my life." —1 Kings 19:4 (KJV)

Now watch what God does.

God does not lecture him about discipline. God does not accuse him of spiritual failure. God sends an angel with food and tells him to sleep. Twice. Only after Elijah's body is cared for does God speak to his heart.

The order matters. Physical depletion required physical remedy before spiritual dialogue could take root. God dignified fatigue. He treated it as reality, not rebellion.

If God responded to Elijah's exhaustion with bread and rest, you can stop repenting for needing both.

And if you think Elijah is an exception, remember Jesus in the boat.

The Son of God—sinless, fully obedient, perfectly aligned with the Father—slept so deeply that a storm did not wake Him. The Gospel writers mention it casually, but the detail is loud. Jesus honored the boundaries of His humanity. He ate. He sat by wells. He withdrew from crowds. He rested without apology.

If the sinless Son embraced fatigue without shame, something is wrong with the man who believes he must transcend it.

This is the part many men resist: flesh is finite—and that is not sin.

Paul wrote that the outward man is perishing even while the inward man is renewed day by day (2 Corinthians 4:16). He did not describe bodily limits as a spiritual defect. He described them as part of life in a fallen world. We carry treasure in jars of clay. The cracks don't corrupt the treasure; they frame it.

Spiritual maturity cannot be measured by perpetual vigor. If that were the standard, aging would be disqualifying. You can steward your health wisely, but you cannot outwork humanity. When you try, you do not become holy— you become exhausted while pretending not to be.

This is where many men fall into a counterfeit gospel.

Not always a heresy spoken aloud, but a pressure absorbed slowly: optimize everything. Sleep less. Grind more. Be sharper. Be faster. Be relentless.

Christian language can even be layered over it—"for the Kingdom," "for my family," "for excellence." God becomes the fuel additive in a performance engine.

But the gospel is not selfimprovement. It is surrender.

The Spirit strengthens you for obedience—not for spectacle. When energy fades, that is not a malfunction in God's design. It is the design reminding you to return to the Source. A man was never meant to be his own supply line.

Now, to be clear: fatigue can coexist with sin. Sometimes men are tired because they ignore God's rhythms, overcommit out of pride, or feed their minds on things that drain rather than restore. When that is the case, repentance involves realignment.

But even then, the exhaustion itself is not the sin. The disorder is.

Other times fatigue is simply the cost of love and obedience. A father with a newborn. A caregiver. A man walking through grief. A man providing through hard seasons. Jesus Himself collapsed under the weight of the cross—not because He mismanaged His schedule, but because redemption required strain.

So tiredness is not always correction. Sometimes it is consequence—holy consequence—of living faithfully in a broken world.

Here is another hard truth: exhaustion, while not sinful, is fertile soil for temptation.

When the body is depleted, shortcuts speak louder. That's not an excuse; it's a warning. Scripture shows it repeatedly: men make foolish decisions when they are weary, hungry, isolated, and drained. Jesus told His disciples to watch and pray so they would not enter temptation, and then found them sleeping. He didn't deny their humanity—He simply acknowledged the danger of ignoring it:

"the spirit indeed is willing, but the flesh is weak." —Matthew 26:41 (KJV)

Tiredness is not failure. But it is a crossroads.

Attend to it—or you will eventually sin to escape it.

So what does strength actually look like?

Not the capacity to avoid fatigue. The courage to admit it. And the wisdom to respond correctly.

Isaiah says it plainly:

"Even the youths shall faint and be weary, and the young men shall utterly fall: But they that wait upon the LORD shall renew their strength." —Isaiah 40:30–31 (KJV)

Even the young men fall. Scripture assumes it. The difference is not who gets tired—it is who knows where strength is renewed.

They that wait upon the LORD renew their strength. Waiting is not laziness. It is dependence. It is refusing to treat personal capacity as the source. It is choosing connection over pride.

An eagle does not flap itself into power. It rides the current. The lift comes from outside itself. Its job is to spread wings and remain positioned. That is the picture of a man learning dependence: not manufacturing strength, but receiving it.

So when fatigue shows up—today or next month—do not interpret it as condemnation. Do not scold yourself for being human. Bring the weariness to God. Adjust what needs adjusting. Rest when rest is needed. Seek help when help is wise. And remember that none of this disqualifies you.

Strong men still get tired. Wise men stop pretending they don't.

In the next chapter we will confront the phrase that often blocks this wisdom: *"I got this."* It sounds responsible, even righteous. But it quietly trains men to live as their own source.

And that is always where exhaustion begins.

Chapter 4 - The Myth of "I Got This"

Lie: Depending on God means I've lost control.

Truth: Control is the illusion that keeps men from rest—and keeps God from leading.

The Silent Nod We Give Ourselves

There is a silent nod many men give themselves at the start of the day: **I got this.**

You can hear it in the way a man exhales when the meeting ends and everyone files out. You can sense it in the way he checks his pockets—keys, phone, wallet—before stepping into the night. You can feel it when he lies awake mapping tomorrow like a general marking troop movements.

It usually isn't said out loud. Volume would betray the insecurity it's trying to cover. Instead, it's a quiet vow—an internal handshake between a man and his desire to be enough.

In the last chapter we named something men often hide: fatigue. Strong men still get tired. But between the moment you feel tired and the moment you ask for help, a sentence whispers, *Come on. You can handle this one more time.*

That sentence sounds harmless. Responsible, even. Left unchecked, it becomes a myth: that a man's worth rises or falls on how long he can keep carrying everything alone.

And because the world applauds the man who never drops anything, the myth feels like truth.

How Control Masquerades as Strength

Control is seductive because it dresses like responsibility.

To be clear, responsibility is holy. Eden blossomed under stewardship. Men were created to work, lead, cultivate, protect. Initiative and diligence are not sins to repent of. Your family and your community do not benefit from a man who confuses spirituality with passivity.

But stewardship and control are not the same thing.

Stewardship has a relational posture—open hands beneath the care of God. Control curls those hands into fists.

Control says, *If I release my grip, everything I love will unravel.* Stewardship says, *If I release my grip into God's hands, everything I love is safer than it is with me.*

Control moves at the speed of anxiety. Stewardship walks at the pace of trust.

And because trust feels slower, control often feels stronger. Men mistake urgency for wisdom. They applaud the late-night email, the skipped rest day, the always-on availability. Every time they meet that standard, the inner voice throws confetti: *See? You did it again. You proved you're enough.*

But biblical strength is never measured by how much pressure you can hide. It is measured by how willingly you remain connected to God.

When Competence Crowds Out Connection

Competence isn't evil. The world needs men who can solve problems and take initiative. But competence becomes dangerous when it quietly replaces communion.

That shift usually doesn't happen through rebellion. It happens through efficiency. A man still believes in God. Still reads Scripture. Still attends church. He simply begins to rely on God less in the ordinary moments because he has learned he can manage them himself.

Prayer becomes power steering fluid: useful when the wheel gets stiff, unnecessary when the road feels smooth.

And this is the deception: self-reliance can look like maturity. It can look like leadership. It can even look like faithfulness—until something shakes the system hard enough to reveal what's actually been powering it.

Jesus' words in John 15 are not poetic decoration. They are diagnosis:

"I am the vine, ye are the branches… for without me ye can do nothing." — John 15:5 (KJV)

A branch doesn't die in dramatic fashion. It dries out slowly. From a distance it still looks attached—same shape, same bark, same position. But life stops flowing long before the leaves turn brown.

That is what self-reliance does to men. It doesn't instantly ruin them. It quietly dries them out.

The Unseen Tax of Carrying Everything

Every "I got this" moment charges a tax against the soul that doesn't come due immediately.

Some men carry that debt for years. They juggle deadlines, provide steadily, show up to everything, volunteer at church, fix the leaky faucet on Saturday, and still look fine from the outside. They assume they're thriving because accomplishments keep stacking and people keep praising.

But the debt compounds.

One day it shows up in a doctor's office as chest tightness. Another day in a counselor's room as tears that feel embarrassing. Another day in a kitchen when a spouse says, *You're here, but you're not home.*

They search for catastrophe and find none—only a thousand tiny withdrawals of trust. The tax of self-reliance isn't always a crash. It's often a slow repossession of joy.

And joy is usually the first thing control steals.

A Plumb Line for the Soul

A carpenter doesn't rely on what looks straight. He measures.

A simple plumb line—weight on the end of a string—reveals what the eye can miss. A wall can look square until it's tested.

Self-reliance is the same. It can look noble until God measures it.

And the measurement is simple: **Where do you instinctively go first?**

To prayer—or to control? To God—or to strategy? To surrender—or to tightening the grip?

This is where many men get uncomfortable, because the answer reveals how deeply the "I got this" myth has set up residence.

King Asa's Subtle Shift

Scripture gives a sober example in King Asa.

Asa started well. When an enormous army came against Judah, he cried to God:

"LORD, it is nothing with thee to help, whether with many, or with them that have no power… we rest on thee." —2 Chronicles 14:11 (KJV)

God delivered him.

But later, when another threat rose, Asa stopped resting on the Lord and started resting on leverage. He took silver and gold and bought help through an alliance. Politically, it worked. Spiritually, it was a shift in source.

A prophet confronted him:

"Because thou hast relied on the king of Syria, and not relied on the LORD thy God…" —2 Chronicles 16:7 (KJV)

Asa didn't become an atheist. He didn't renounce faith. He simply stopped relying.

That's the warning for men like us. Most men don't fall by denying God. They fall by slowly replacing reliance with competence.

Pride in Sunday Clothes

Pride rarely roars. It usually smiles.

That's why "I got this" is so insidious—it wears Sunday clothes. It serves. It gives. It appears strong. It even thanks God publicly while privately insisting on control.

Deep down, pride prefers a God who cheers from the stands rather than one who calls the plays. If God is a spectator, you can credit Him after the touchdown. If He is Lord, you must run His routes, trust His cadence, and obey even when the route makes no sense.

The enemy doesn't need to make a man rebellious to weaken him. He only needs to make him independent.

What Surrender Is—and Isn't

Surrender is not resignation.

Some men hear "trust God" and assume it means disengage, stop trying, let life happen. That isn't surrender. That's passivity dressed up as spirituality.

Surrender is active. It plans with open hands. It works hard without worshiping effort. It obeys without insisting on control.

It is not the end of engagement—it is the end of illusion.

Control says, *Outcomes depend on me.* Surrender says, *Obedience belongs to me; outcomes belong to God.*

That is wisdom. Not weakness.

Practicing the Open Hand

Here is a simple practice that exposes where a man truly lives.

Tomorrow morning, before your feet hit the floor, sit on the edge of the bed and place both hands on your thighs, palms down. Feel how natural that posture is. Palms down is control. It is ready to grab, brace, push.

Now turn your palms up.

Nothing in your life changes in that moment—alarm still ringing, schedule still waiting—but something in you shifts. That posture is a confession: **I am a receiver before I am a producer.**

This isn't magic. It's alignment. A physical reminder that strength is not something you manufacture. It is something you receive from God.

Learning to Be Carried

Children understand something men resist.

When a child is hurt or tired, he raises his arms. No apology. No speech. Just a simple assumption: *my father is near, and his strength is for me.*

Many grown men apologize to God for asking small help. They act as though dependence is permitted only after they've proven effort.

Jesus says the opposite:

"Except ye… become as little children, ye shall not enter into the kingdom of heaven." —Matthew 18:3 (KJV)

Childlikeness is not immaturity. It is trust without performance.

Spiritual maturity does not graduate a man into independence. It sinks his roots deeper into reliance.

Trading the Illusion for the Vine

You'll leave this chapter and face the same bills, responsibilities, and pressures that waited while you read. The question is what story you carry back into them.

You can clutch the myth of "I got this" until your knuckles whiten and your heart caves in. Or you can trade that illusion for the Vine that never withers.

Part I has done one thing: it has told the truth about men and limits.

- You were built to need God.
- Burnout is a signal, not failure.
- Strong men still get tired.
- And "I got this" is not strength—it's the doorway to self-reliance.

Now we step into Part II—the heartbeat of this book.

Not a God who supplements your strength. A God who becomes your strength.

Turn the page with open hands.

Part I Closing Reflection — The End of Self-Reliance

By now, something should feel unsettled.

Not alarmed. Not condemned. But quietly disrupted.

Part I has not tried to fix you. It has not handed you techniques, habits, or formulas. It has done something more fundamental—and more uncomfortable. It has questioned assumptions you may have lived on for decades without ever naming.

You were built to need God.
Burnout is not failure—it is a signal.
Strong men still get tired.
And "I got this" is not strength; it is an illusion.

Taken individually, each truth sounds reasonable. Taken together, they dismantle a way of life many men have mistaken for maturity.

What Part I has exposed is not a lack of effort, discipline, or responsibility. Most men reading this do not suffer from passivity. They suffer from **misplaced strength**—from carrying life as though self-reliance were a virtue God admired rather than a habit Scripture warns against.

From the beginning, this book has insisted on a reframing: limits are not defects. They are design. God did not create men to be self-sustaining engines. He created them to be dependent, connected, and sustained. The modern myth of masculine independence may earn respect in boardrooms and locker rooms, but it slowly starves the soul.

Burnout is what happens when design is ignored long enough to protest. It is not proof of weak faith; it is evidence of prolonged self-reliance. Fatigue is not an indictment; it is information. It tells the truth about the body and the soul when pride refuses to.

And still, many men resist that truth—not because they are arrogant, but because they are afraid. Afraid that loosening control will lead to collapse. Afraid that dependence will expose weakness. Afraid that surrender will cost them credibility, momentum, or identity.

So they whisper, *I got this*, and keep going.

Part I has named that phrase for what it is: not confidence, but quiet pride. Not courage, but fear disguised as competence. Not faith, but independence wearing church clothes.

This is where many men expect rebuke.

Instead, Scripture offers clarity.

God does not shame men for being dust. He formed them that way. He does not scold the weary for being tired. He invites them to rest. He does not withdraw from those who reach their limits. He meets them there.

The problem is not that men work hard.
The problem is that they work *alone*.

Part I ends here intentionally—at the edge of self-reliance. Not with answers, but with exposure. Not with relief, but with honesty. Because nothing meaningful can be built until illusions are dismantled.

If you feel slightly off-balance right now, that is appropriate. A foundation has been disturbed. Old definitions of strength no longer hold. Familiar instincts have been questioned. That discomfort is not weakness—it is awareness.

And awareness creates a choice.

You can attempt to rebuild self-reliance with better habits, cleaner schedules, or more disciplined effort. Many men do. It works for a while.

Or you can step into a different way of living—one where strength does not originate with you at all.

That is where Part II begins.

Part II does not offer God as a supplement to your existing strength. It does not frame grace as a backup plan or a recharge station for exhausted men who intend to return to independence as soon as possible.

It introduces a harder, freer truth:
God does not strengthen you so you can remain self-reliant.
He strengthens you so you can remain dependent.

That shift changes everything.

It changes how you interpret weakness.
It changes how you carry responsibility.
It changes how you endure.
It changes how you lead.
It changes how you rest.

Strength, as Scripture defines it, is not something you summon. It is something you receive. Not once, but continually. Not in emergencies only, but as a way of life.

Part I has cleared the ground.

Part II will build on it—not by demanding more from you, but by revealing more of the God who meets you exactly where your strength ends.

Turn the page ready—not to prove, perform, or push—but to learn what it means to live by **Strength Beyond You**.

PART II — Strength That Doesn't Come From Me

Lie: God's strength is a backup plan – it is the source

Chapter 5 - Strength Beyond Me

Lie: God helps me after I've done my part.

Truth: God's strength is not supplemental—it is foundational.

A Doorway, Not a Detour

You are reading this chapter because something in you already knows the truth: the well you've been drawing from is not bottomless.

Maybe the previous chapters helped you name the fatigue. Maybe you arrived here already past the point of naming it. Either way, you have stood in the light long enough to see the limits of human strength without flinching.

And now, something shifts. Not in your circumstances, but in your posture.

You step through a doorway.

The threshold is narrow—the width of a single confession:

My best is not enough, and that is not a flaw in me.

On the other side is not collapse, but clarity. Not passivity, but a shift in source. Strength does not disappear—it relocates. From you, to Christ.

This chapter is not about adding God to your existing effort. It is about replacing the engine entirely.

Most men try to live like hybrid vehicles—running on their own power until the battery drains, then switching to God as backup. But the kingdom does not run on hybrid strength. It runs on surrender.

The Verse We Thought We Knew

"I can do all things through Christ which strengtheneth me." —Philippians 4:13 (KJV)

Few verses have been worked harder and understood less.

We've treated it like a motivational slogan—something to shout before effort, not confess during surrender. The verse ends up fueling ambition rather than redefining dependence.

Paul wrote it from prison.

No platform. No momentum. No illusion of control. He wasn't charging hills—he was waiting on a verdict that could end his life. And in that context he says he has learned contentment. Not victory. Contentment.

"I know both how to be abased, and I know how to abound… I am instructed both to be full and to be hungry." —Philippians 4:12 (KJV)

Then comes verse 13.

In other words: **I can endure lack. I can steward abundance. I can walk faithfully whether circumstances cooperate or collapse—through Christ who continually strengthens me.**

This is not self-confidence. It is source clarity.

The grammar matters. Paul isn't saying Christ gave him strength once. He's describing ongoing infusion. Strength is happening *to him*, not being summoned *from him.*

Paul is not the engine. He is the vessel.

Strength as Source, Not Supplement

Most men treat God like an enhancement.

They plan. Decide. Commit. Then ask God to bless what they've already chosen. Divine strength becomes a booster rocket—helpful when things get heavy, unnecessary when they feel manageable.

That's not dependence. That's delegation.

Scripture never presents God as an accessory to human effort. He is the source of life itself. When we reverse that order, exhaustion is inevitable.

You were never meant to run on your own reserves with occasional divine refills. You were meant to live in continuous reliance, like a branch drawing sap moment by moment from the vine.

When Jesus says, "Without me ye can do nothing," He doesn't mean *less.* He means *nothing of lasting value.*

Motion can continue. Activity can look impressive. But life drains.

Self-sufficiency can mimic fruitfulness for a season. But only for a season.

Why Dependence Feels Like Loss

Dependence feels threatening because men are trained to equate control with strength.

Control feels responsible. It feels adult. It feels safe. Letting go feels reckless—like surrendering competence, leadership, or identity.

But control is an illusion.

You do not control outcomes. You manage obedience.

Outcomes have always belonged to God. Dependence doesn't remove responsibility—it removes the lie that responsibility equals sovereignty.

Jesus doesn't invite you to stop working. He invites you to stop carrying the weight alone.

"My yoke is easy, and my burden is light." —Matthew 11:30 (KJV)

The work remains. The distribution changes.

Borrowed Strength Is Not Weak Strength

Some men fear that living Christ-powered will make them passive, hesitant, or disengaged. Scripture shows the opposite.

Dependence produces liberated obedience.

When strength doesn't originate in you, failure no longer threatens identity. Success no longer inflates ego. Energy becomes sustainable because it isn't self-generated.

You still plan. You still lead. You still act.

But you do so without the corrosive pressure of self-sufficiency.

The difference is subtle but seismic:

- Anxiety gives way to steadiness
- Hustle gives way to obedience
- Performance gives way to presence

Borrowed strength is not weak strength. It is the only strength that lasts.

The Weight Was Never Yours

Here is the simplest diagnostic in this chapter:

If the weight feels crushing, it probably doesn't belong on your shoulders.

Christ-powered living doesn't remove difficulty. It removes misplacement.

The load is shared. The pace is set by Someone who sees the whole field.

When strength is borrowed, you stop pretending you own it. You stop apologizing for needing it. You stop hoarding it for emergencies.

You breathe.

Redefining "All Things"

"All things" does not mean endless achievement.

It includes obscurity. Loss. Waiting. Seasons where effort doesn't yield visible reward.

Christ's strength does not guarantee outcomes— **it guarantees faithfulness.**

Sometimes strength looks like endurance. Sometimes restraint. Sometimes obedience without applause. And sometimes it looks like stopping.

Paul's confidence was not that he would always succeed— but that Christ would always supply what obedience required.

Standing in the New Source

This chapter is not asking you to feel different. It's asking you to live sourced differently.

Strength beyond you does not always feel dramatic. Often it feels ordinary—but without panic.

The miracle is not intensity; **it is sustainability.**

Part II will continue to unfold what this kind of strength looks like in practice—especially when grace is misunderstood as a contingency plan instead of the atmosphere of life with God.

For now, let this settle:

You do not need to prove strength. You need to receive it. And the Source has never stopped offering it.

Chapter 6 - Grace Is Not a Backup Plan

Lie: *"Grace is for failure, not for daily living."*

Truth: *Grace is the operating system, not the emergency exit.*

When You Only Call the Tow Truck After the Crash

The highway was clear at dawn, and I had somewhere to be. I eased the truck onto the interstate, confident in the engine under the hood and the coffee in my cup. Halfway through the drive a light blinked on—low oil pressure. I noticed it. I chose to ignore it. I had work to finish, people to meet, a schedule already behind.

Besides, the truck had never failed me.

A mile later the engine coughed, lost power, and rolled to a stop on the shoulder. Smoke drifted from under the hood while commuters whipped past. Only then did I call for help. The towtruck driver climbed down, wiped grease on his coveralls, and shook his head.

"You kept driving after the light came on."

That sentence lands harder than it should because it names a pattern most men recognize.

We notice warning lights—fatigue, irritability, numbing habits, thinning joy—but we keep moving. We silence the dashboard of the soul with caffeine, distraction, or grit. Only when something seizes do we dial heaven's roadside assistance and hope God still answers.

We treat grace like a spare tire buried beneath the jack instead of the fuel coursing through the engine.

Chapter Five established that God's strength is foundational, not supplemental. This chapter goes one layer deeper: strength is delivered through grace. Grace is not Heaven's emergency exit. It is the operating system. The atmosphere. The unseen infrastructure without which nothing runs.

You were never meant to ration grace for moral collisions. You were meant to live on it.

The Default You Were Born Without

The night my first son arrived, the nurse swaddled six pounds of squirming life and placed him in my arms. He could do nothing but inhale, exhale, and cry. Yet as I stared at him, I realized how much I expected from myself. I had a mortgage, a marriage, a calling—and now a human who could not feed himself.

No one handed me extra strength when they handed me that child. They handed me need.

Every man is born with need but without the resources to meet it. Adam woke to a world already humming with provision—rivers flowing, fruit bending branches, oxygen filling lungs. Everything required was already supplied. Nothing was earned.

That is grace in seed form: God acting kindly before man contributes anything.

Somewhere between Eden and adulthood we trade default dependence for selfmanufactured competence. We collect credentials, accounts, and approval. We convince ourselves we can furnish what our souls crave—meaning, forgiveness, rest—through effort and control.

We try to install righteous software onto hardware that never carried it. The system crashes. We reboot. We crash again.

Grace is not an upgrade you purchase in the app store of religion. It is the factory setting.

Sin corrupted the hard drive. Salvation reinstalls the system. Every sunrise is a fresh login. Every breath is a line of code written by a God who knows we cannot run the program alone.

Why We Wait for the Wheels to Fall Off

Most men approach grace the way they approach doctors—after pain becomes intolerable. We were trained in selfreliance long before theology ever touched us.

"Be a man." "Figure it out." "Don't bother people."

We reach for the toolbox first, prayer last. We promise ourselves we'll slow down after this season ends, once the kids get older, once the numbers stabilize. Only when anxiety, betrayal, or failure buckles our knees do we whisper, *Lord, help.*

Peter modeled the instinct. When Jesus walked on water, Peter stepped out in borrowed courage. As long as his eyes stayed on Christ, the surface held. When the wind slapped his face, he reverted to muscle memory—calculate, control, survive. He sank fast.

Only then did he cry out.

We shake our heads at Peter, but we repeat him daily on dry land. We receive grace, divert our gaze, and operate on fumes until circumstances outmuscle us.

Grace requested only in crisis does not build resilience. It guarantees collapse.

No soldier enters combat assuming he'll requisition ammunition after the first volley. Grace is provision stocked in advance—not rations begged for under fire.

What Grace Actually Is

Grace is more than unmerited favor. It is unrelenting supply.

It is God's settled disposition to do good to His children at His own expense, continuously. Forgiveness glitters at its center, but grace does far more. It powers obedience. Fuels endurance. Stabilizes leadership. Nurses grief. Rewrites desire.

Paul told the Corinthians, "By the grace of God I am what I am, and His grace toward me was not in vain." Grace shaped his identity, energized his effort, and produced fruit—yet Paul adds, "I worked harder than all of them—yet not I, but the grace of God that was with me."

Grace worked harder than Paul did.

That sounds mystical until you notice it in real life.

Grace is the patience you didn't have until the Spirit interrupted midargument. Grace is clarity arriving in prayer when yesterday's fog still clings. Grace is restraint that keeps your finger hovering over "send" until anger drains from the email.

Grace does not pamper laziness. It empowers faithfulness.

It does not erase responsibility; it infuses it with Christ's life.

You still wake up, lead meetings, speak truth, reconcile conflict. You just do it like a branch drawing sap from a vine—not like a cut flower trying to stay alive by sheer willpower.

Grace in the Mundane Monday

When I served on staff at a small church, Monday was trash day. I resented dragging bins to the curb after Sunday's emotional exhaustion. Sermons preached. Tears prayed through. Couldn't someone else handle garbage?

One humid morning, midcomplaint, I sensed a quiet nudge: **This is also holy.**

That sentence both broke something and healed something.

Grace does not wait for pulpits or crises. It inhabits voice mails, spreadsheets, traffic, grocery lines, diapers, and dental appointments.

Grace refuses compartments. It turns beige routines into sanctuaries.

You don't escape your life to experience grace. You inhale grace to live the life you already have.

Responsibility Is Not Rivalry

Some men bristle here. If grace carries me, am I responsible for anything?

That fear misunderstands grace.

Grace enlarges capacity without inflating ego.

Picture a father helping his toddler build a block tower. The child places bricks while the father steadies the base and supplies more pieces. When the tower stands, the child squeals, "I built it!" The father laughs.

Grace works like that.

You work out your salvation because God works in you. You discipline your body—but not by power native to your veins.

Grace and grit are not rivals. Grace animates grit.

Passivity isn't surrender. Selfsufficiency isn't responsibility.

Grace produces action saturated with humility and gratitude.

Training Your Appetites on Grace

The enemy of grace is not sin first—it is selfsufficiency. And detoxing from selfsufficiency takes rhythm, not resolve.

Three simple practices recalibrate the soul:

Each morning, before screens light up, I pray aloud: *Father, everything I need today is already in You.*

Throughout the day, when stress spikes, I pause and breathe: *Grace. Right now.*

At night, I review the day and name where grace showed up—often where I missed it in real time.

These are not formulas. They are touchpoints.

Over time, dependence becomes instinctive. Grace stops feeling theoretical and starts feeling atmospheric.

Grace or Burnout—Your Choice

Burnout is rarely just a scheduling problem. It's a theological one.

Plates multiply because we assume spinning them is our job alone. Grace exposes motives beneath overload: approval hunger, fear of irrelevance, messiah complexes masquerading as faithfulness.

When grace is backup, burnout is inevitable. When grace is operating system, capacity flexes without collapse.

You may still work hard in certain seasons—but with inner rest. Saying no becomes holy. Results stop naming you.

I once asked a CEO to write a resignation letter—not from his job, but from acting as savior of the company. He signed it and placed it in his Bible. Weeks later he said numbers still mattered, but they no longer owned him.

That's grace at work—breaking the illusion of indispensability.

Grace Is the Face God Turns Toward You

Numbers blesses God's people this way: "The Lord make His face shine upon you and be gracious to you."

Grace is not only what God does. It is how God looks at you.

Prior to Jesus' miracle, the Father expressed pleasure. Ministry stemmed from approval, not towards it. This same gaze is upon you through Christ. Performance cannot diminish it, and failure cannot revoke it.

Grace anchors worth beyond output— and paradoxically produces better obedience, because fear no longer drives the engine.

Conclusion: Already Supplied

Tonight, when you turn out the light, your future will sleep. God will not.

He will keep heartbeats steady and galaxies spinning. By morning, mercy will already be waiting.

Grace is not dessert for those who finish their vegetables. Grace is breakfast before labor.

Tomorrow's chapter will explore the unsettling paradox this truth unlocks: God's power shows brightest not when strength peaks—but when weakness admits need.

For now, rest here.

You are not behind. You are not running out. You are already supplied.

Chapter 7 - Power Perfected in Weakness

Lie: Weakness disqualifies me from usefulness.

Truth: Weakness is where God's power is most clearly seen and least confused with ego.

A Quiet Bridge from Grace to Power

Chapter 6 set the record straight: grace isn't the tow truck you call after the engine smokes. It's the operating system you're meant to run on every day.

And yet here's the question men don't always say out loud:

If grace is real and present, why do I still feel so weak? Why does faith sometimes feel like a trembling hand instead of a clenched fist?

Most men assume weakness is evidence something isn't working—our discipline, our prayer life, our masculinity, our "spiritual maturity." But Scripture keeps telling a different story:

Grace does not eliminate weakness. Grace inhabits it.

God's power doesn't replace frailty. It flows through it.

What we try to escape, God often chooses to employ.

Weakness is not the enemy of strength. It is the doorway to it.

The Thorn That Reframed the Whole Conversation

The clearest explanation of this comes from a man who had every reason to sound invincible.

Paul writes to the Corinthians—people who were impressed by charisma, polish, and spiritual "proof." He tells them about visions, revelations, and extraordinary ministry. Then he drops the part that makes achievers squirm:

To keep him from becoming conceited, a "thorn in the flesh" was given. He pleaded three times for God to remove it.

And God answered—not with relief, but with a sentence that rearranges how strength works:

"My grace is sufficient for you, for My power is made perfect in weakness."

That's not inspirational wallpaper. That's a demolition charge.

God didn't deny Paul's pain. He didn't tell him to "toughen up." He didn't shame him for asking.

But He refused to remove what would keep Paul dependent—because the bigger danger wasn't discomfort. The bigger danger was conceit. Not the thorn, but the ego that grows when a man feels unstoppable.

So God reframed the thorn as a stage:

This is where My power will show up so clearly that you won't be able to confuse it with you.

Paul's response is the part that feels almost offensive to modern instincts:

"Therefore I will boast all the more gladly about my weaknesses, so that Christ's power may rest on me… For when I am weak, then I am strong."

He isn't romanticizing suffering. He's describing a spiritual reality:

Weakness creates vacancy—space in the soul where God's strength can actually land.

Pride fills every room. Weakness clears one.

Weakness Has Two Faces

Before we go further, we have to name something men often muddle.

There's **honest frailty**, and there's **indulgent selfpity**.

Honest frailty says, "I'm limited, and I need God," and then it moves toward obedience with open hands.

Selfpity says, "I'm limited, so nothing is expected of me," and it settles into resignation.

Both can sound similar in conversation. The difference is in the fruit.

Paul's thorn didn't make him quit. It made him cling.

It didn't shrink his calling; it purified it.

If "weakness" becomes the excuse to disengage from what God has clearly assigned, it isn't humility—it's avoidance dressed in sadness.

God doesn't glamorize weakness. He uses it. But He uses it in surrendered hands.

Why Weakness Is Actually a Gift to a Man

Calling weakness a gift can sound insulting—until you see what it protects you from.

Weakness does at least three things men desperately need:

1.It preserves intimacy.

Nothing exposes prayerlessness like the moment selfreliance stops working. Weakness drives you back to the Source—not as a concept, but as survival.

2.It keeps the spotlight clean.

When a man never appears needy, people start confusing the man with the mission. Weakness prevents idolatry—both yours and theirs. It quietly declares: **This isn't built on my horsepower.**

3.It produces resilient obedience.

Men who learn dependence early don't collapse when life turns. They bend without snapping because they already know where strength comes from.

Weakness doesn't feel good. It just happens to be useful.

Jacob's Limp: The End of Outrunning God

If Paul gives us theology, Jacob gives us a picture you can't unsee.

Jacob spent his life avoiding vulnerability—manipulating, scheming, staying one step ahead. Then one night God wrestled him into honesty, and Jacob left with a limp.

That limp wasn't punishment. It was preservation.

It meant Jacob could no longer confuse survival skill with spiritual strength. He had to walk slower. He had to live more aware. He had to remember, with every uneven step, that blessing comes from God—not from being clever enough to control outcomes.

A limp is what happens when God refuses to let you keep calling your coping mechanisms "strength."

The Modern Thorn: Image Management

Most men today aren't wrestling God at a river. They're wrestling the fear of looking weak.

We curate. We edit. We "fine" our way through checkins.

We maintain the brand: competent, unbothered, always good, always steady, always in control.

But image management is a brutal religion. It taxes the soul daily.

It turns every critique into a threat. Every compliment into a sedative. Every mistake into panic.

And it quietly teaches you the lie you've been swallowing for years:

If people see my weakness, I lose value.

Paul's thorn exposes the opposite: weakness doesn't erase usefulness—it clarifies where the power is coming from.

You don't have to announce every struggle to everyone. But you do have to stop pretending you're bulletproof.

The branch that insists it's not a branch cuts itself off from the vine.

Weakness Doesn't Cancel Calling—Denial Does

Here's what actually disqualifies men over time: not weakness, but **unowned weakness**.

A man who refuses limits eventually pays for it somewhere:

- in secret coping
- in irritability at home
- in a body that forces rest
- in relationships that stop trusting him
- in leadership that turns controlling because it's terrified

Limits ignored don't vanish. They just collect interest.

Owning weakness is what creates sustainable obedience. It forces honest pacing. It invites community. It decentralizes responsibility. It keeps a man human—and therefore usable.

The Cross: Weakness That Won

To truly understand that God embraces weakness, look to the cross.

Despite its appearance of chaos and defeat, the cross is referred to in Scripture as a display of God's power.

That moment of apparent weakness was actually the turning point in which evil was defeated.

God doesn't simply tolerate weakness, He uses it for redemption.

Therefore, your weakness is not a flaw in the gospel narrative, but a crucial aspect that reveals the true power of the gospel.

A Simple Practice: Stop Treating Weakness Like a Fire to Hide

This week, try one small, stubborn act:

When weakness shows up—fatigue, fear, uncertainty—don't patch it immediately with performance. Don't cover it with humor. Don't outrun it with productivity.

Name it to God plainly:

"I feel weak here. I need You here."

Then obey the next right thing at the pace of grace— not the pace of panic.

Weakness is not your identity. It's just the doorway where power tends to enter.

Turning Toward What's Next

By now the pattern should be getting clear:

Grace is the operating system. Weakness is not a disqualifier—it's the stage. Power shows up where ego can't take credit.

That leads to the next question:

How do you live day after day like a receiver, not an owner? How do you stop treating strength like private property?

Next chapter, we'll step into that: the reality that everything you call "mine"—breath, energy, capacity—is borrowed… and the Father's supply doesn't run dry.

Chapter 8 - Borrowed Breath, Borrowed Strength

Lie: "What I have, I earned."

Truth: Every breath is a gift. Strength was never owned—only stewarded.

The Echo of the Last Chapter

Paul's confession about the thorn still lingers. We just traced how weakness became the doorway through which God's power entered his life—how the place that felt like disqualification became the place where Christ was least confused with ego.

If that's true, it raises a harder question:

Why do you and I still move through most days as if strength were something we own outright?

I have a hunch: we forget the most basic fact of our existence.

You are renting every heartbeat. Every lungful is borrowed. The power that surges through tendons, the clarity that solves problems, the stamina that gets you out of bed to provide—none of it originated in you.

You steward it for a while, then you hand it back.

That sounds poetic until Monday morning shows up yelling through an alarm clock. Then it sounds… un-American.

We are products of a culture that reveres the self-made man—the lone wolf who bootstraps his way from nothing to empire. Even in church circles, testimonies can subtly hinge on how hard we worked after we found Jesus. The narrative stays tilted toward us.

Borrowed breath flattens that narrative. It relocates the credit. And if we let it, it frees us from shouldering a weight we were never designed to own.

Standing on Someone Else's Oxygen

I was twenty-four the first time I watched a ventilator keep someone alive.

A friend's father collapsed with viral pneumonia. The machine forced air into his lungs while he lay unconscious, chest lifting with mechanical precision. I remember standing there, staring at the tube snaking down his throat, listening to the hiss and click that timed every breath.

It struck me with uncomfortable clarity: a silent motor fifty inches from his head was now doing what he had done effortlessly since birth.

All his life, oxygen had slipped in and out of his chest without him noticing. But the moment the machine unplugged, the story changed.

On the drive home I had a ridiculous thought: **every one of us is on a ventilator.**

Ours is just invisible—woven by God into the atmosphere. In Eden, He gathered soil and breathed. He never retracted that breath. He never revoked the loan. He simply kept supplying air and called it normal.

If tomorrow God turned off the flow, our chests would fall still before the news cycle could notify us.

We are that dependent. That fragile. That thoroughly sustained.

The difference between that hospital room and my ordinary Tuesday wasn't dependency. It was visibility.

The Myth of Ownership

Somewhere between childhood and your first mortgage, you were sold a story called ownership.

Banks reinforced it. Jobs reinforced it. Even some pulpits reinforced it.

You might have signed the contract without realizing it: **If I produce enough, I earn the right to keep what I have.**

Scripture dismantles that premise with one sentence:

"The earth is the Lord's, and the fullness thereof; the world, and they that dwell therein."

God claims title to the planet—and then slides in the detail we'd prefer to skip. He owns every inhabitant too.

That means you are included in the "fullness." Breath, IQ, muscle mass, résumé, opportunities, influence, longevity—file it under the Lord's.

Yet we still grip time, talent, and treasure with a proprietary fist.

Why? Because ownership gives the illusion of control.

If the strength is mine, I get to allocate it, flaunt it, spend it however I deem worthy. If the strength is on loan, I become a steward.

Stewards answer to the Owner. They manage the house by Someone else's priorities.

And that's the part that unnerves the self-made ego: **stewardship removes final veto power.**

But stewardship also delivers a quiet, muscular peace.

When ultimate responsibility shifts off your shoulders, your soul ligaments loosen. You can work hard without worshiping work. You can plan diligently without panicking when plans unravel. You can lead without acting like the Messiah of the operation.

Ownership creates insomnia. Stewardship makes space for sleep.

Dust, Breath, and the Return Policy

Genesis insists man is dust, animated by divine breath. Ecclesiastes closes the loop: one day the dust returns to the earth and the spirit returns to God who gave it.

Life is a temporary marriage of soil and soul, orchestrated by a faithful Lender.

If that sounds morbid, it's only because we rarely meditate on borrowings.

Imagine picking up a rental car. You adjust mirrors, crank the seat back, and merge onto the freeway. After a few hours you almost forget you don't own the vehicle—until a rock cracks the windshield.

Suddenly you remember paperwork. Liability. The day your credit card statement will reflect what happened.

Mortality is the crack in the windshield that reminds us we don't own the car.

We might keep it for eight decades. We may accessorize it with degrees, job titles, rank, retirement portfolios, and "good years."

But eventually the body returns to dust and the spirit returns to God.

Recognizing loan status doesn't shrink vision; it sharpens it.

You drive differently when you remember Whose name is on the title.

When the Loan Masquerades as Salary

I once mentored a young executive who believed eighty-hour weeks were the price tag on success. He slept five hours, lived on energy drinks, and skipped church because "Sunday is prep day." For a while, the equation seemed to work. Quarterly numbers rose. His boss applauded. His phone never slept.

Then a routine physical found blood pressure levels that belonged to a man twice his age.

He laughed—until a personal alarm woke him at three a.m. with chest pain sharp enough to convince him he was dying. Ambulances. EKGs. A stern physician. And finally, reality:

the strength he spent like salary was only a loan.

He said it out loud in the hospital: "I forgot I was mortal."

Mortality has a way of exposing ownership myths. That heart scare was grace.

He downsized his schedule, reoriented priorities, and discovered that the God who owns his body also owns the outcomes of every board meeting.

In releasing ownership, he regained life.

Entitlement or Gratitude

Borrowed breath leaves us with two possible postures.

Entitlement says: "Of course I get tomorrow."

Gratitude whispers: "I can't believe I get another sunrise."

Entitlement fuels hurry, comparison, and the chronic angst that you're always one accomplishment behind. Gratitude slows the pulse. It magnifies simple beauty. It turns ordinary corridors into sanctuaries.

I learned this in airports.

During a season of frequent travel, I began feeling entitled to on-time departures. Any delay became personal insult. One stormy night in Denver every gate slid from green to red. Thousands of passengers groaned while crews fought for traction on the runway.

I had zero control, yet my internal monologue argued with weather patterns like storms respond to human ego.

A few rows away, an elderly veteran in a wheelchair hummed softly. Every few minutes he tipped his head upward—like the steel roof was transparent—and said, "Thank You, Lord, for one more day."

I asked why he was so calm.

He said, "After Vietnam, every extra sunrise feels like bonus time."

He carried a theology of borrowed breath that trumped inconvenience. I carried entitlement disguised as efficiency.

One of us worshiped. The other stewed.

The Freedom of Stewardship

Stewardship may sound like suffocation—another spiritual chore stuffed into an already crowded calendar.

It's the opposite.

When ownership shifts to God, unmanageable burdens exit your jurisdiction.

Consider the father worried he must protect his teenage son from every cultural snare. Ownership screams, **If I parent perfectly, my boy will turn out right.**

Stewardship sighs, **God, You lent me this child. I will guide him, but You are his Keeper.**

That shift is the difference between insomnia and rest.

Or the entrepreneur who feels fifty families hang on his decisions. Ownership says, **If I fail, I destroy them.**

Stewardship says, **Lord, You own the cattle on a thousand hills and the market I'm competing in. Teach me diligence; protect me from messiah complexes.**

God doesn't delegate sovereignty. He shares responsibility.

You still parent. You still lead. You still train.

You just do it from the settled place of a steward who knows where limits end and Providence begins.

Practicing Borrowed Strength

Theology is sterile until it becomes Tuesday.

So how do you practice borrowed breath without drifting into dreamy mysticism that ignores normal life?

Start small. Start conscious.

When your alarm rings, inhale before you scroll. Recognize oxygen as an allotment, not an automatic refill. Offer the day back to the Giver.

At breakfast, taste the food instead of shoveling it while skimming headlines. Remember: photosynthesis, supply chains, farmers you will never meet—all converged so protein could hit your plate. Gratitude becomes easy when it becomes specific.

In conversation, resist the reflex to dominate. Remember the voice leaving your vocal cords is sustained by wind from God's lungs. Let that humble your tone, even in disagreement.

When you lift weights or run trails, relish the miracle of muscle fibers firing under electrochemical commands. Not everyone can stand unaided. Borrowed strength should birth praise before pride.

These habits seem small, but God invented compound interest. Stewardship grows in increments—then shows up sturdy when crisis hits.

Men who cultivate daily awareness of borrowed breath tend not to implode when pressure spikes. They've spent years practicing release.

Sabbath: Scheduled Surrender

Sleep is a nightly Sabbath—engineered surrender. While you drool unconscious, you return control to God.

Weekly Sabbath is the amplified version. You quit working, the earth keeps spinning, and the lesson is obvious:

the universe does not require your supervision.

I once told a mentor I felt guilty resting because the church I served had so many needs. He laughed and said, "Brother, God ran His kingdom long before you were born. He'll keep running it while you nap."

That's not laziness. That's accurate theology.

Jesus and the Borrowed Boat

One afternoon, Jesus taught crowds so large they pressed Him against the shoreline. He spotted an empty fishing boat and asked the owner to push off a little from land. From that borrowed boat, Christ declared eternal truth.

Afterward, He filled the same boat with more fish than the nets could hold.

Notice the order: **Jesus borrowed, then blessed.**

He still does it that way.

He borrows your voice, your schedule, your resources—and if you hold them loosely enough for Him to use, He fills them with significance you could never manufacture.

But if you cling too tightly, you might preserve the boat and miss the miracle.

When Strength Fades Anyway

Even the most faithful steward faces decline. Aging knees creak. Vision blurs. Reaction time slows. Our culture often sidelines older men, but Scripture crowns them with wisdom.

A retired missionary once told me, "I can't build churches in the jungle anymore, but I can still build prayer walls."

From a nursing-home recliner he prays for hours. Staff slide notes under his door requesting intercession. His voice is raspy, but heaven counts it thunder.

Your capacity may contract through illness, age, or unexpected loss. That doesn't revoke stewardship; it reshapes it.

You trade sledgehammers for shepherd staffs. Spreadsheets for supplication.

The loan adjusts terms, but it doesn't expire until God recalls it.

Conclusion: Setting Down What Was Never Mine

We began with weakness—how it can become a doorway for power. We end deeper: strength itself was borrowed long before it was drained or abundant.

The breath you're drawing while reading these words is on loan from heaven, and one day it will cycle back to its Source.

What does that mean for tomorrow's meetings, diapers, workouts, deadlines?

It means you can enter each task without pretending to be sovereign. You can laugh at interruptions, knowing the Owner is still on site. You can quiet the inner drill sergeant that barks, "Produce or perish," because your identity was sealed long before your résumé had ink.

Borrowed breath also sets up the next movement of this book: **daily dependence**. If everything is on loan, wisdom is staying close to the Lender—not as a panic response, but as a steady way of life.

For now, pause. Exhale the air that never belonged to you. Inhale the mercy waiting at the edge of your nostrils. Whisper gratitude.

And rest—because the One who keeps lending breath has never defaulted on generosity yet.

PART III — Walking in God's Strength Daily

Lie: Dependence is passive.

Chapter 9 - Daily Dependence Is a Discipline

Lie: "Leaning on God means doing less."

Truth: Dependence is active obedience, practiced daily.

Yesterday's Lesson, Today's Invitation

In the last chapter we stood still long enough to remember that every pulse in our wrists is borrowed. The oxygen in our lungs, the stamina in our muscles, the doorways we walk through before eight a.m.—none of them originate with us. They arrive on loan.

That realization humbles a man in the quiet moments. But it also raises an awkward question once the crisis settles and life looks manageable again:

What do I do with that truth tomorrow morning when my calendar is full, coffee is brewing, and nothing looks dire?

Most of us acknowledge dependency instinctively when something hurts—when a diagnosis lands, when a kid breaks our heart, when money evaporates without raising its hand first. We hit our knees, sometimes literally.

But when the bleeding stops and the inbox fills again, reliance slides to the margins. We drift back into the cycle we know too well:

manage, maintain, impress, repeat.

I have lived that pattern more times than I want you to know. Seasons of desperation have driven me to prayer before dawn, and seasons of calm have drifted me back to polite nods toward God somewhere around lunch. It's not always rebellion. It's muscle memory.

Self-reliance is the default setting of fallen humanity. Dependence must be chosen—then chosen again—until it becomes how a man breathes.

That is why we have to talk about discipline.

When Need Is No Longer Obvious

My friend Marcus builds homes for a living. He tells me the most dangerous moment on any jobsite is not when the foundation is poured or when the roof is lifted into place. It's the first week after the walls go up.

Before drywall, everyone walks carefully. The framing is visible. You can see what will hold you and what won't. But once the sheetrock is hung and painted, danger hides. A misplaced step finds drywall instead of a beam, and a man ends up in the living room below.

Comfort disguises risk.

The spiritual life works like that. When crisis exposes our limits, we pray with intensity because we can see the open space under our feet. Once stability returns, we assume the footing is secure. We don't feel less Christian. We simply feel less needy—which is usually the first lie that walks back through the door.

Daily dependence is the deliberate refusal to let visible stability replace invisible support. It's the quiet confession that even when the floors look finished, there is still only air under our soles unless God holds the house.

A Week Practicing Dependence

Dependence sounds noble when we talk about it in theory. It sounds spiritual when it's framed as posture or principle. But if dependence is truly a discipline, it must survive contact with a normal week—one that includes meetings, irritation, temptation, fatigue, and moments where nothing feels especially spiritual at all.

Let me show you what this looks like lived, not explained.

Monday — When urgency tries to lead

Emails stacked up before breakfast. A meeting I didn't want to lead had been rescheduled earlier, and the internal pressure to "be on" kicked in before my feet touched the floor. My instinct was speed—coffee faster, shower shorter, prayer postponed until later.

Dependence interrupted that reflex.

I sat on the edge of the bed and said out loud, **"Father, if I run today on my own strength, I will make a mess of it. I'm giving You the lead before I give anyone else my attention."**

Nothing mystical followed. No emotional surge. But the pace shifted. Not the schedule—the pace.

Dependence doesn't always remove pressure; it recalibrates how you carry it.

Tuesday — When things feel manageable

The day felt manageable, which is precisely when dependence feels unnecessary. That's the danger zone. I skipped morning prayer entirely and told myself I'd reconnect later.

By midafternoon my patience thinned, my tone sharpened, and I caught myself rehearsing conversations I hadn't even had yet—always a sign I've taken the wheel back.

I paused in the parking lot before driving home and laughed quietly at myself. "So this is what self-sufficiency looks like after six hours."

I prayed a short, honest reset. Not repentance drenched in shame—just reattachment. That evening went differently, not because circumstances changed, but because the source did.

Wednesday — When temptation whispers escape

Not the dramatic kind, but the subtle pull toward numbing. Scroll longer. Stay distracted. Avoid the conversation that requires attention.

Dependence here looked like restraint, not action. I turned the phone face down. I asked God for strength to stay present instead of escaping.

That prayer cost me comfort. It gave me peace.

Thursday — When failure shows up

I snapped at someone I love. I defended myself instead of listening. Dependence didn't prevent the misstep—but it shortened the distance back.

I apologized quickly. That alone told me something had changed.

When dependence is practiced daily, pride doesn't get time to build infrastructure.

Friday — When nothing dramatic happens

No breakthroughs. No disasters. Just steadiness.

I realized something important: **dependence doesn't make life dramatic—it makes it durable.**

That week didn't transform my circumstances. It transformed my reflexes.

And reflexes shape lives.

This is how discipline forms—not through heroic moments, but through repeated returns.

Dependence Is Not Passive

Here's the common misunderstanding: men hear "dependence" and picture weakness, like leaning on a wall because your legs can't do their job. We confuse dependence with passivity—like trusting God means sitting on the couch waiting for a miracle while life collapses around you.

But biblical dependence isn't a nap on the battlefield. It's more like a soldier staying in radio contact with command.

He still moves. He still fights. He still makes decisions.

But he refuses to operate like he is alone.

Dependence is not doing less. It is refusing to do anything disconnected from the Source.

It's active obedience. Practiced daily.

The Shape of Early-Morning Surrender

A mentor once told me, **"If you don't decide who you are before breakfast, the rest of the world will decide for you by lunch."**

He wasn't talking about motivational mirror speeches. He was talking about surrender.

I wake up early. I used to do it because pastors are supposed to model discipline. Now I do it because my soul limps by noon if I don't.

I pour coffee, open Scripture, and before I read a verse, I exhale a sentence:

"Father, I cannot live today without You."

No music. No goose bumps. Just honesty.

Some mornings I feel that statement in my bones. Other mornings it feels like I'm reading a sign out loud. But the point is not emotion. The point is alignment.

A branch doesn't attach itself to the vine through feelings. It remains connected because life depends on it.

When you begin your day with surrender, you decide whose strength will handle the emails that have not been typed yet, the temptation that has not knocked yet, and the tension that has not flared yet.

That decision needs to be made early—because once the phone starts buzzing, the vote is usually over.

The Theology of Manna

God trained Israel in dependence with food that spoiled overnight. Manna gathered on Monday would rot by Tuesday.

Every sunrise required fresh gathering. That wasn't poor food preservation. That was divine education.

Israel had lived four hundred years under Pharaoh. Their provision came from human storehouses—even when those storehouses were cruel. God had to retrain them to look up each morning instead of looking back to the system that enslaved them.

And I know men—myself included—who secretly wish the manna principle had exemptions for savings accounts, graduate degrees, good health insurance, and stable seasons.

We believe in daily bread theoretically, but we still want a pantry stocked three months deep so we can feel secure if God decides to take a day off.

He doesn't take days off. And He won't apologize for designing dependence into His economy.

Yesterday's intimacy will not sustain today's obedience. Yesterday's grace was real, but it was not meant to become today's substitute for communion.

Gather again.

Naming Your Need

Dependence becomes practical the moment you put vocabulary around what you lack. Vague prayers produce vague reliance.

The soul loves generalities: "Lord, be with me today."

That's not sinful. It's just shallow.

He is already with you. The question is whether you will admit the places you can't stand without Him.

A few years ago anxiety started visiting me at two a.m. I would jolt awake with my mind sprinting through worst-case scenarios—budget collapse, children harmed, leadership failure, a heart that quits early.

I tried to fight the spiral with positive thinking, but positivity doesn't outmuscle darkness at two a.m.

A counselor asked me, **"Have you told God exactly what you're afraid of, or have you only prayed for the feeling to go away?"**

That question exposed me.

My prayers were polite: "Give me peace." But what I meant was, "Make this stop."

Naming the dread felt embarrassing—until I did it.

And when I started whispering,

"Father, I'm afraid my leadership will fail. I'm afraid my children will be hurt. I'm afraid I can't carry this,"

something shifted.

I wasn't offering a devotional platitude. I was handing Him an itemized list of weaknesses He already saw but waited for me to acknowledge.

Need that is hidden can't be surrendered.

When Dependence Breaks—and How It Restarts

Here is the part most men won't say out loud: even when you commit to daily dependence, you will still fail at it.

You will wake up intending to lean on God and end the day having leaned mostly on yourself. You will pray in the morning and still react in the afternoon. You will know better and still choose control.

If your definition of dependence requires a clean record, you will abandon it the first time pride flares or patience snaps.

That is where shame enters.

Shame whispers, **You knew what to do. You didn't do it. Now clean yourself up before you go back to God.**

Pride nods along. Handle it. Fix it. Don't make a big deal out of it.

Together they keep you disconnected longer than the failure ever did.

I learned this the hard way.

There was a season when I was intentionally practicing daily surrender—early mornings, Scripture open, honest prayer. Then one afternoon I reacted sharply to a colleague. It wasn't explosive, just clipped enough to wound.

I justified it immediately. He should've known better. I'm under a lot of pressure. I'll deal with it later.

By evening the justification had curdled into heaviness. Prayer felt awkward. I avoided it. That avoidance lasted three days.

Nothing dramatic happened in those days. No moral collapse. Just a slow tightening—irritation at home, impatience in traffic, a faint edge of self-protection creeping into every interaction.

I told myself I was "busy." The truth was simpler: I was embarrassed to reattach.

That is pride's favorite move. Not rebellion—delay.

When I finally sat down, I didn't confess eloquently. I said, **"Father, I've been pretending I can't come back until I do better. That was never Your rule."**

The relief was immediate—not because I felt forgiven (though I was), but because the pressure to perform dissolved.

I hadn't broken dependence by failing. I had broken it by withdrawing.

Here is the crucial distinction:

Dependence doesn't fail when you stumble. It fails when you refuse to return.

Shame wants you to believe God is disappointed. Pride wants you to believe you're capable of fixing it solo.

Both lies keep you self-reliant longer than necessary.

Daily dependence includes daily resets.

Sometimes that reset is confession. Sometimes it's apology. Sometimes it's sitting quietly and admitting, **I tried to carry this again.**

What matters is speed, not ceremony.

The longer you wait, the more control calcifies into posture.

I've learned to recognize the warning signs:

- defensiveness instead of curiosity
- justification instead of listening
- prayer shrinking into silence

Those are not signals to try harder. They are invitations to reconnect.

Think of dependence like breathing. You don't punish yourself for forgetting a breath—you inhale again.

You don't replay the lapse; you restore oxygen.

The discipline is not flawless breathing. It's uninterrupted return.

Pride says, **I'll reattach once I've stabilized.**

Grace says, **Reattach so you can stabilize.**

One of the most freeing realizations of my adult faith was this: **God is not monitoring your dependence to grade it. He is supplying it to sustain you.**

That means you don't restart dependence tomorrow. You restart it now.

The Saved Cut — Three Rhythms of Daily Dependence

Now we get practical—not with formulas, but with rhythms. Because dependence has to fit into a man's real life: jobsite boots, hospital waiting rooms, school pickup lines, board meetings, text threads, budgets, temptations.

Here are three rhythms—morning, middle, and evening—that have helped recalibrate my default settings over time. They are not magic. They are muscle memory for the soul.

1. Morning — Declare the Source before the world declares the scoreboard

Before screens glow and tasks start yelling, I speak one sentence aloud:

"Father, everything I need today is already in You."

It's short enough to pray half-asleep. It's disruptive enough to rewire pride.

This is not me trying to convince God. It's me refusing to lie to myself.

The day will tempt you to live like the strength is yours. This sentence tells the truth before the lie gains momentum.

2. Middle — Interrupt self-reliance in real time

Somewhere around mid-morning, the day starts leaning on your neck. That's when I practice what I call a micro-reset.

When I feel the pulse quicken—an email, a tense conversation, a meeting I don't want—I pause for a breath and whisper:

"Grace right now."

Sometimes I even put my hand on my chest, not for drama, but for awareness. My body often recognizes overload before my theology does.

That one phrase re-centers me. It reminds me I'm not performing alone. I'm not carrying outcomes. I'm not sovereign.

It takes ten seconds. And it saves hours of damage.

3. Evening — Review and release

At night, before sleep, I rehearse three things:

- Where I saw grace today (even if I missed it in the moment)
- Where I need to confess (without excuse, without self-hatred)
- What I cannot control tonight (and must hand back)

Then I pray something like:

"Father, I release what I can't fix. Watch the hallway while I sleep."

Sleep is the most honest act of dependence most men still practice. You go unconscious and the universe refuses to collapse.

That's God preaching while you drool.

Over time these rhythms do something subtle but powerful: they train you to recognize dependence not as an emergency reaction, but as a daily way of living.

Abiding in Micro-Moments

I used to believe spiritual depth required long, uninterrupted hours. Sometimes it does. But Jesus also revealed kingdom power in motion— walking roads, sitting at wells, attending dinners, moving through crowds.

Abiding isn't only a morning block on your calendar. It's the habit of returning to God in small moments throughout the day:

- "Help me listen" before your teenager talks.
- "Guard my eyes" before you open your laptop.
- "Give me patience" before you walk into the house after a long commute.
- "Thank You" when laughter breaks out at the table.

None of these prayers are long enough to impress anybody, which is exactly why they build a man.

When the Day Derails

Dependence isn't proven by a peaceful sunrise. It's proven by how quickly you reset after peace collapses.

When frustration tightens your chest, pausing for sixty seconds to inhale, exhale, and say,

"Father, I hand this to You,"

can prevent hours of wreckage later.

Sometimes that reset looks like apologizing before the argument escalates. Sometimes it looks like closing the laptop so you don't reply while angry.

Surrender almost always costs you your preferred pace. But it returns more strength than it asks for.

Conclusion — Tomorrow's Assignment

Dependence won't cancel your mortgage. It won't raise your kids for you. It won't magically delete responsibility.

What it does is place each responsibility back where it belongs—inside the grip of God—while you steward it from a position of connection instead of panic.

But another question naturally emerges:

How do you know which weights God is asking you to steward and which ones you've claimed without invitation? Where's the line between faithfulness and overload?

That's where we're going next.

For tonight, gather tomorrow's manna. Name your real need. Practice the rhythms—morning, middle, evening.

And rest. The same God who keeps lending breath will be awake while you sleep, already preparing strength for first light.

Chapter 10 - When God Carries What I Can't

Lie: If I don't carry it, it won't get done.

Truth: God carries what no man was built to survive holding.

From Posture to Weight

Daily dependence trains a posture.

This chapter asks a harder question: **what exactly are you carrying?**

Once a man begins to lean on God intentionally, another realization surfaces—often uninvited. Some of the strain he feels isn't from obedience. It's from ownership. Not everything pressing into his chest was assigned by God. Some of it was assumed quietly, baptized with good intentions, and carried long past what his frame could bear.

That realization rarely comes during prayer. It comes in hallways, parking lots, and hospital waiting rooms. It comes when a teenager's voice cracks. When payroll is due. When the phone lights up again and again with problems that refuse to respect dinner time.

The weight shows up first. The question follows:

Is this mine to carry—or am I doing God's job for Him?

The Invisible Weight Room

Most men live in a private gym no one ever visits. We rack burden after burden onto the bar and tell ourselves we're fine.

One more rep. One more season. One more push.

- The sick parent.
- The drifting marriage.
- The responsibility to keep everyone calm.
- The unspoken belief that collapse is not an option.

Individually, these burdens may not seem overwhelming. But it's the combined weight and the lack of acknowledgment that takes its toll. The struggle to keep it all together consumes us more than the actual tasks. The endless preparation, the worry, and the sleepless nights all add to the strain.

Faith doesn't protect men from this weight. Sometimes it increases it— because responsibility gets confused with righteousness. We assume that spiritual maturity means carrying more, longer, and quieter.

Scripture tells a different story.

The holier a man becomes, the quicker he recognizes the limits of his shoulders— and the faster he transfers weight to the only One who does not strain under it.

Broad Shoulders, Wrong Load

God designed men to carry real responsibility. Strength is not the problem. Misallocation is.

Adam was given meaningful work—cultivate, keep, steward—but never autonomy. God retained the heavy lifting: sustaining creation, defining good and evil, guarding the boundaries. The moment Adam assumed authority God never assigned, his shoulders buckled.

That pattern hasn't changed.

What breaks men isn't usually the work God gives them. It's the outcomes God never asked them to guarantee.

- Proving worth.
- Managing everyone's emotional weather.
- Securing results only God can control.

Strength becomes the argument: **If I can carry it, I should.**

That math ruins men.

How Men Confuse Calling with Control

Most men don't wake up intending to carry what God never assigned. We arrive there through a series of quiet substitutions.

We confuse **responsibility** with **control**. We confuse **love** with **outcome management**. We confuse **calling** with **personal indispensability**.

The shift is subtle enough that it feels virtuous.

- A man is entrusted with a family, so he assumes he must guarantee their happiness.
- A leader is given influence, so he assumes he must prevent all failure.
- A provider sees needs, so he assumes the results rest squarely on his shoulders.

Scripture never makes those assumptions.

God assigns **faithfulness**, not outcomes. He entrusts **presence**, not omnipotence. He calls men to **stand in the gap**, not **be the gap**.

Yet pride quietly reframes the job description. Pride says, **If this fails, it says something about me.** Fear adds, **So I'd better not let it fail.**

That's when the weight shifts from obedience to ownership.

Ownership is intoxicating because it masquerades as importance. You feel needed. You feel essential. You feel irreplaceable.

But that feeling is not calling—it's pressure. And pressure is a terrible compass.

Here's a diagnostic question that rarely lies:

If this collapsed tomorrow, would I grieve—or would my identity collapse with it?

Grief is human. Identity collapse reveals unauthorized weight.

God does not entrust His glory to your adrenal system. If a burden requires you to violate Sabbath, ignore prayer, silence wise counsel, or live perpetually clenched, it has already drifted outside divine assignment.

God's work may stretch you, but it will not require you to impersonate Him.

Jesus never once panicked about outcomes. He wept. He raged at injustice. He carried sorrow. But He never hustled to secure results the Father had not given Him to secure.

When crowds demanded more miracles, He withdrew. When disciples misunderstood, He taught and moved on. When betrayal came, He did not scramble to preserve reputation.

Control was never His posture.

If you feel crushed, it may not be because the work is too heavy. It may be because you're carrying the wrong kind of weight.

The Unequal Yoke We Resist

Jesus doesn't promise a weightless life. He promises a different yoke.

A yoke pairs two animals—one seasoned, one learning. The stronger carries most of the pull. The other contributes but never dominates.

Jesus' invitation is not to disengage, but to reposition.

Most of us pray for strength to carry our existing yoke instead of asking whether it's His.

That sounds humble. It's usually pride in religious clothing.

Christ never asked you to carry the full weight of your family's future, your organization's survival, or another adult's spiritual outcome.

He asked you to walk beside Him—obedient, present, attentive— while He bears what would crush you.

What Unauthorized Weight Costs

Carrying what isn't yours rarely causes immediate collapse. It erodes instead.

- **Emotionally**, you live tight—irritable or numb.
- **Relationally**, you withdraw from anyone who threatens your fragile composure.
- **Spiritually**, prayer becomes transactional.
- **Physically**, your body protests quietly until it doesn't.

I learned this during a season of unexpected growth in a nonprofit I led. Opportunity multiplied faster than infrastructure. Instead of slowing down, I sped up—convinced faithfulness meant endurance.

Sleep shortened. Joy vanished. Scripture became a checklist.

One night my daughter said, **"I like the daddy who doesn't look angry at his phone."**

That sentence exposed what prayer had not.

I had asked God to bless the work— and then tried to carry the blessing alone.

Repentance looked practical: delegation, boundaries, unglamorous conversations. More importantly, it meant reclaiming space where God— not adrenaline—set the pace.

The load didn't disappear. But it redistributed.

And redistributed weight feels lighter.

Discerning What's Yours to Carry

This isn't guesswork. God provides markers.

First—Scripture. God will not assign burdens that require chronic distance from Him or neglect of those you're called to love. Intensity may season a calling. Perpetual absence corrupts it.

Second—fruit. God-given weight produces peace beneath pressure. Self-assumed weight produces restlessness, defensiveness, and scarcity thinking.

Third—community. Trusted men see what you normalize. Pride hides. Wisdom invites witnesses.

Fourth—the body. Pain is not always attack. Sometimes it's instruction.

Finally—resistance. God leads. He doesn't shove. If every door requires force, pause.

These aren't rigid formulas. They're plumb lines.

They help you ask, **Is this obedience—or is this me auditioning for God's job?**

Release Without Abandonment

Setting down weight is not quitting. It's transferring.

Picture loosening your grip—not throwing the rope away, but opening your hand until God takes the dominant pull. You still walk. You still work. But the tension no longer originates in you.

Release costs admiration. It purchases peace.

It often looks unimpressive: smaller calendars, slower growth, quieter obedience. Heaven seems comfortable with that trade.

Peter still walked out of prison— but the chains fell without his strength.

Jehoshaphat still showed up— but God fought the battle.

Partnership doesn't remove effort; it removes impossibility.

From Pack Mule to Pilgrim

Men trapped under unauthorized weight become pack mules—valued for capacity, discarded when legs falter.

Men who transfer weight become pilgrims—still moving, still responsible, but defined by direction and companionship rather than load.

Pilgrims travel lighter. They rest when told. They trust provision ahead.

One builds monuments to endurance. The other builds altars to grace.

Closing: A Lighter Lift

Some of what presses into you tonight is yours to steward. Some of it never was.

The invitation is not to drop responsibility, but to place it correctly—inside the strength of God rather than on the limits of flesh.

As we move forward, we'll look at what sustained endurance looks like once weight is rightly shared. For now, listen to the ancient command that still rescues men from collapse:

Cast your cares upon Me—for I care for you.

Feel the bar lift. Stay in step. Let God carry what no man was built to survive holding.

Chapter 11 - Strength to Keep Going

Lie: Endurance comes from willpower

Truth: Endurance comes from staying connected to the Source

The Long Middle

Relief is not the end of the journey. It is the beginning of endurance.

In the last chapter, you set down weights that were never yours to carry. Some pressure lifted. Your shoulders dropped. Your breath deepened. But the road ahead did not shorten. Life did not pause out of respect for your surrender. Work still demands attention. People still need you. Temptation still whispers. Faith still requires movement.

And it's right there — in the quiet after release but before renewal — that endurance begins to take shape. Not in the dramatic moments, but in the long middle where obedience feels repetitive and strength feels quiet.

This chapter is not about powering through. It is about remaining.

The Miles Nobody Cheers For

I once ran a halfmarathon. The first mile was loud — cowbells, signs, familiar faces shouting my name. The last mile was desperate — legs burning, lungs bargaining, the finish line finally visible.

But the middle miles were silent.

No cheers. No landmarks. Just breath, pavement, and the question: *Will you keep going when nothing feels dramatic?*

Most of life is lived in those miles, and that's where the real work happens. Marriages aren't sustained by weddings and anniversaries alone, but by years of unremarkable faithfulness. Faith doesn't collapse in moments of crisis nearly as often as it erodes during long seasons of sameness. Most men don't quit because they are overwhelmed; they drift because nothing feels urgent enough to fight for.

And drift, left unattended, becomes distance.

Endurance is forged where motivation fades — which leads us to the real problem with relying on willpower alone.

Why Willpower Fails

Willpower is a limited resource. It feeds on visible progress and measurable reward, both of which the kingdom of God often withholds for long stretches. Jesus described growth as yeast in dough, seeds under soil, treasure buried in fields — all slow, hidden processes.

Willpower thrives on applause. Endurance survives without it.

That is why Jesus never told His disciples to try harder. He told them to abide.

Branches don't generate strength. They remain attached. When they disconnect, effort increases and fruit disappears. When they remain, life flows quietly — even when nothing looks impressive.

And that quiet flow is what most men miss, because they're waiting for something louder — a surge, a spark, a second wind.

The Myth of the Second Wind

Many men approach faith like endurance sports: push until empty, wait for a surge, repeat. But Scripture does not promise frequent second winds. It promises daily breath.

Paul described being pressed, perplexed, persecuted, struck down — yet never abandoned. Not rescued from pressure, but sustained within it. Endurance, for him, was not an adrenaline rush. It was oxygen.

Jesus called it a yoke — not because the load vanished, but because the pull was shared. The weight still existed. The strain no longer crushed.

And if that sounds unrealistic, Jesus Himself shows us what this looks like in practice.

Jesus Modeled Staying Power

The Son of God withdrew often. He rested. He prayed. He left crowds when momentum peaked. He slept during storms. He refused to let demand define direction.

If endurance were about output, Jesus failed the metrics. If endurance is about connection, He perfected it.

He remained so closely tethered to the Father that exhaustion never severed purpose. That is not mysticism. That is model.

And Paul, chained in a cell, learned the same secret.

Paul's Secret Was Not Temperament

Philippians was written in chains. No stage. No strategy. No control. Yet Paul spoke of contentment — not because circumstances improved, but because his Source never changed.

"I can do all things through Christ who strengthens me" was not a slogan of dominance. It was a confession of dependence.

Endurance is not stubborn personality. It is practiced access.

And that access reshapes the way we breathe, pray, and move through ordinary days.

Breathing Instead of Performing

Abiding is not complicated; it is constant.

Prayer becomes breath instead of performance. Scripture becomes nourishment instead of homework. Community becomes oxygen instead of obligation.

Neglect rarely kills immediately — it suffocates gradually.

Daily dependence trains internal supply lines so that when pressure comes, strength arrives without panic. No applause. No surge. Just capacity.

And sometimes, endurance looks less like action and more like waiting without resentment.

When Nothing Changes

Some endurance is not about effort but waiting without bitterness.

Habakkuk prayed, "How long?" God answered not with a timeline but with perspective. The righteous live by faithfulness — by staying tethered when circumstances refuse to budge.

Joy in those seasons is not denial. It is defiance.

It says: *God's character does not fluctuate with outcomes.*

And if you need a picture of what that looks like in flesh and bone, I think of a man named Marcos.

Endurance in Flesh and Bone

I once worked alongside a man named Marcos who slowly lost physical strength to disease. As his mobility declined, his influence multiplied. He talked to Jesus more because he had to. His dependence deepened his joy.

His endurance was not heroic grit. It was unclogged access.

When he died, the room overflowed with people shaped by a man whose strength diminished while his connection intensified.

His life preached a sermon his body could no longer speak.

And the truth is, most endurance is built long before moments like his — in the quiet routines no one sees.

Ordinary Tuesdays Build Eternal Strength

Scripture celebrates quiet perseverance more than spectacle.

The church grew not just through miracles but through meals, prayers, generosity, and daily obedience. Kingdom endurance is built in routines no one records.

Showing up. Forgiving quickly. Working honestly. Praying tired prayers. Remaining.

Heaven sees what Tuesday hides.

And when those Tuesdays accumulate, something subtle begins to shift inside you.

How to Recognize God's Strength at Work

God's strength rarely feels loud. It feels sustainable.

When you respond with patience instead of panic. When you recover quicker from discouragement. When obedience costs less drama. When prayer interrupts anxiety midsentence.

That is endurance.

And it leads us to the simplest, most freeing truth of all.

Closing: Staying Attached

You don't need to sprint. You don't need to impress heaven. You don't need to finish strong today.

You need to stay connected.

Endurance is not built by gritting teeth but by remaining rooted. The Vine does the heavy lifting. The branch just stays.

The middle miles are holy ground. Keep breathing. Keep attached. The strength to keep going is already flowing.

Chapter 12 - When Obedience Requires More Than Energy

Lie: If I'm tired, I should step back from obedience.

Truth: Obedience is not powered by energy—it's powered by trust.

A Quiet Turn in the Road

By the time you finished the previous chapter, something likely settled in you. You recognized that endurance is not forged by willpower but sustained by connection. Strength flows from remaining attached to God, not from grinding harder.

That realization brings relief—but it also exposes a harder question, one that does not arrive gently:

What happens when God asks you to obey after your energy is gone?

Not when you're inspired. Not when the path is clear. Not when your reserves feel adequate.

But when obedience costs sleep, reputation, comfort, momentum, or certainty.

This is the point where many men quietly renegotiate discipleship. Not out loud. Not formally. Just internally.

Surely God understands. Surely rest means retreat. Surely obedience can wait until I feel stronger.

But Scripture tells a different story.

There are moments when obedience does not wait for energy to return—**because obedience itself becomes the place where God supplies what you no longer have.**

This chapter is written for that moment.

When Willpower Isn't Enough

For years I believed exhaustion was primarily a logistical failure. If I managed time better, if I planned smarter, if I protected margins more aggressively, I would always have enough strength to do what God asked.

That belief survived until obedience demanded more than efficiency could provide.

A mentor finally said what no productivity system ever would:

"You cannot schedule your way into unlimited obedience. At some point, you have to be carried."

That sentence offended my pride before it healed my soul.

Peter learned the same lesson after resurrection morning, standing ankle-deep in Galilee with empty nets and exhausted arms. He wasn't lazy. He wasn't disobedient. He was simply depleted.

Then a voice from shore gave an instruction that made no practical sense:

"Cast the net on the other side."

Peter did not generate new strength. He did not summon motivation. He listened—and obeyed.

The net filled beyond his ability to lift.

Alignment did what effort could not.

That is the pattern. Obedience does not begin with more energy. It begins with trust that listens even when strength is low.

Obedience Becomes Costly

Obedience is cheap until it threatens something you love.

I learned that one Thursday night, standing in my kitchen long after the house had gone quiet. The Spirit pressed a simple command:

Call Marcus.

Marcus and I had parted under tension. Calling meant reopening something unresolved. It also meant sacrificing the little rest I had left. I tried bargaining—tomorrow, an email, a text—but the prompting did not lift.

So I called.

Ninety minutes later, after apology and silence and mutual relief, I hung up the phone drained and strangely full. It was 1:17 a.m. My body was depleted. My soul was settled.

Obedience did not restore energy. It restored alignment.

That distinction matters. Obedience often drains the body while feeding the spirit. When that happens, you are standing on holy ground.

Obedience Requires Presence, Not Performance

Jesus never separated obedience from presence.

He did not issue assignments and disappear. He paired command with companionship.

That is where many men falter—not because the command is unclear, but because they attempt obedience in isolation.

We know what Scripture says. We understand what faith requires.

But we try to obey without remaining near the One who empowers obedience.

When that happens, fatigue masquerades as discernment.

We assume the command must be wrong because strength is gone. But the command was never the problem. **The separation was.**

Gethsemane: The Pattern We Avoid

Gethsemane reveals the anatomy of God-powered obedience.

Jesus told the truth about His weakness: **"My soul is overwhelmed."**

He asked honestly for relief: **"If it is possible, let this cup pass."**

Then He surrendered beyond energy: **"Not My will, but Yours."**

Only after surrender came strength.

We want that sequence reversed. Strength first. Surrender second.

God refuses.

He gives strength to surrendered men, not to self-protective ones.

If the sinless Son of God did not obey by adrenaline, what makes us think we can?

When Exhaustion Becomes a Teacher

Some men interpret fatigue as failure. Scripture treats it as information.

Elijah collapsed not because he disobeyed, but because he obeyed long enough to run out of himself.

God did not shame him. He fed him. He let him sleep. Then He spoke.

God does not discard tired servants. He restores them.

But restoration does not always mean removal of the assignment. Sometimes it means renewed trust inside the assignment.

Stories from the Trenches

Sophia, a single mother in our church, works two jobs and serves on the prayer team. She once told me, **"I resigned internally before I ever resigned externally."**

God did not remove her from service. He carried her through it.

Joel, trapped in addiction for decades, did not break free through discipline. He broke free when obedience reduced him to tears and dependence replaced strategy.

Neither story ends with ease. Both end with trust.

Obedience without energy is not heroic. It is honest.

Practicing Obedience When Strength Is Gone

This is not a formula. It is a posture.

1. **Name the cost.** Drag it into the light. God works with honesty, not bravado.

2. **Locate the Presence.** Before action, pursue nearness. Obedience without presence becomes performance.

3. **Take one step.** God multiplies loaves, not plans. He strengthens movement, not hypotheticals.

4. **Rest without guilt.** God feeds His servants between assignments. Rest is not retreat—it is replenishment.

5. **Record faithfulness.** Memory fuels future obedience. What God carried you through becomes tomorrow's courage.

These practices do not eliminate fatigue. They prevent despair.

The Quiet Yes

Obedience without energy looks unimpressive.

It looks like showing up tired but truthful. Like choosing faithfulness over applause. Like Jesus whispering *Yes* while everyone else sleeps.

Heaven weighs obedience differently than the world.

And the men who learn to obey when energy is gone often discover something rare:

obedience was never sustained by their strength at all. It was sustained by trust.

Where This Leads Next

If obedience requires trust more than energy, the final question remains:

How do you stay when obedience becomes long, unseen, and unrewarded?

That is the conversation of the next chapter.

For now, rest here. If God is asking you to obey beyond your energy, it is not because He miscalculated. It is because He intends to carry you through what you could never sustain alone.

And being carried is not a concession. It is the way sons walk.

PART IV — Strong Enough to Finish

Chapter 13 — Strength to Stay

Lie: Finishing well means never slowing down.

Truth: Staying requires sustained dependence.

When the Adrenaline Wears Off

Most callings begin with momentum.

You sense God nudging you toward something new—a responsibility, a relationship, a role—and adrenaline floods your system. Vision sharpens. Sacrifice feels noble. You pray more easily. You imagine fruit before thorns.

You start well.

Then days turn into months. Months into years. The shine dulls. The calling doesn't disappear, but it settles into routine. Dust gathers on what once felt electric.

- The children you begged God for now wake you before dawn.
- The marriage you vowed to cherish starts replaying old misunderstandings.
- The ministry that once felt miraculous fills your phone with quiet emergencies.
- The job you prayed into becomes the job that keeps you late again.

And beneath the noise, a question begins to hum:

How long can I keep this up?

In the last chapter, we talked about obedience when energy is gone. But this chapter presses further.

What happens after you obey? After the surge fades? After God doesn't release you, reroute you, or replace you?

This is where staying lives.

Not rescue. Not breakthrough. **The long, faithful middle.**

Staying may be the quietest miracle God ever performs.

Why Quitting Feels So Reasonable

Before we talk about staying, we need to be honest about quitting.

Quitting isn't always rebellion. Sometimes it feels wise.

Exhaustion whispers, *You've given enough.* Comparison sneers, *Someone else would do this better.* Fear mutters, *If you keep going, you'll fail publicly.*

Add those voices together and leaving can sound like discernment.

But quitting for the wrong reasons leaves a residue—a low-grade ache that follows you into the next season. You move on, but something unfinished moves with you.

Years ago, a man stepped away from a small group he led because it never grew. "Someone else can take them further," he said.

No one ever did. Those six drifted.

Years later he told me, quietly, **"I still wonder what would've happened if I'd stayed."**

When God assigns you somewhere, leaving early rarely feels clean. It leaves threads untied—not because you're indispensable, but because obedience was incomplete.

The Illusion of Toughness

Most men assume staying is about toughness.

Clench your jaw. Push through. Endure.

That version of staying works—for a while.

But grit without dependence turns brittle. Grind hardens the soul. Love dries up. Creativity fades. Cynicism moves in.

Biblical staying is not stoic endurance. It is sustained dependence—the same dependence that carried Israel through forty unglamorous wilderness years, that kept Daniel praying when lions circled, that held Paul steady through decades of rejection and imprisonment.

Toughness burns too hot to last. Dependence draws from a fire that never goes out.

Anchors That Hold Over Time

Men who stay do not rely on a single reason. They drop anchors—plural—into bedrock that storms cannot uproot all at once.

These are not techniques. They are relationships. And they hold.

The Anchor of Calling

Paul often introduced himself the same way:

"Paul, an apostle of Jesus Christ by the will of God."

That wasn't branding. It was ballast.

Calling answers the deepest question beneath every quitting fantasy:

Why am I still here? Because God placed me here.

A friend of mine, Malcolm, became principal of a failing inner-city school. Violence was routine. Progress was slow. After year one, the board wanted him out. We sat in a diner over cold coffee when he whispered,

"I know God sent me here. Nothing else explains why I'm still standing."

He stayed.

Year three brought change. Year five produced the district's first valedictorian in forty years.

"You don't walk away from a sending," he told me later.

Calling doesn't remove hardship. It gives hardship meaning.

The Anchor of Communion

Staying is impossible without presence.

Not church activity. Not spiritual productivity. **Presence.**

The disciples endured threats and prisons because people recognized they "had been with Jesus." That nearness marked them.

I learned this during a season when ministry pressure braided with anxiety until my chest ached every morning. Doctors called it stress. I called it Tuesday.

What eased it wasn't strategy. It was unhurried time in the Psalms—not to study, not to prepare, but to be near.

Problems stayed. God drew closer. Their volume dropped.

A man who stays with Jesus never stays alone.

The Anchor of Community

Men who stay do not stay solo.

Moses needed Aaron and Hur. David needed Jonathan. Jesus invited friends into His anguish.

Isolation turns staying into suffering. Community redistributes weight.

I meet weekly with a group of pastors. We start with one question:

"What do you need to say out loud before it sinks you?"

Sometimes the answers are small. Sometimes nuclear.

We pray. We laugh. We leave lighter—not because problems vanished, but because burdens were shared.

Staying requires witnesses.

The Anchor of Hope

Hope keeps staying from becoming a life sentence.

Not optimism. Certainty.

Paul framed suffering inside eternity. John saw a tearless city from exile. Hope stitched their obedience to an ending pain could not cancel.

My grandfather cared for my grandmother through twelve years of dementia. She forgot him. Yelled at him. Wandered at night. He still shaved her face and read Psalms she couldn't comprehend.

"How did you keep going?" I asked.

"One day she'll remember again," he said.

Hope kept him faithful when love alone would've collapsed.

When Staying Looks Like Losing

Here's the truth no one markets: sometimes staying ends in apparent failure.

Jeremiah preached forty years without revival. John the Baptist stayed obedient and died imprisoned. Jesus stayed—and was crucified.

If success is immediate fruit, staying will feel like losing.

Years ago, God asked me, **"If the numbers never grow, am I still worth your yes?"**

Answering yes broke me. It also freed me.

From heaven's view, staying is never wasted— even when outcomes disappear.

Early Signs You're Slipping

Men rarely quit suddenly. They drift.

- Prayer becomes briefing, not communion
- Bitterness replaces burden
- Escape fantasies multiply
- Isolation deepens

These are warnings, not verdicts. Confess them early. Staying requires maintenance.

The Pace of Grace

Grace has a tempo. It is slower than ego.

Jesus rested. Withdrew. Slept mid-storm.

I used to brag about five-hour nights. Panic attacks cured that theology.

Now I schedule silence like oxygen.

You last longer when you stop sprinting for God.

Why God Honors Staying

God calls Himself faithful more than powerful.

When men stay, they mirror Him.

Children learn God's constancy from fathers who keep coming home. Congregations learn trust from leaders who don't vanish when attendance dips. Spouses glimpse covenant from love that remains after novelty fades.

Your staying preaches.

On the Other Side of Staying

Something happens to men who stay.

Fear loses leverage. Love deepens. Authority grows quiet and weighty.

People ask how you lasted.

Your answer is simple: **God kept me.**

A Personal Confession

I almost didn't write this chapter.

Deadlines collided with grief. My father died mid-draft. I told my editor I might quit.

She said, **"The book is about God's strength when yours runs out. Maybe this is part of it."**

So I stayed.

What I learned: finishing wasn't about discipline. It was about discovering the God who writes with trembling hands.

How to Stay Tomorrow

Wake up and talk to God before fear gets first word. Say, **"I'm still here."**

Ask for daily bread, not lifetime clarity. Then show up.

Ignore the scoreboard for a day. Repeat.

Where This Leads

Staying positions you to finish—not collapsed, but carried.

The next chapter explores that final stretch: what it means to finish with God's strength, and why the end often reveals dependence more clearly than the beginning ever could.

For now, plant your feet.

Staying is not stubbornness. It is trust that refuses to walk away.

And God honors men who stay.

Chapter 14 - Finishing with God's Strength, Not Mine

Lie: *"I have to hold on until the end."*

Truth: *God holds us through the end.*

The Hand-Off

You and I have already had a long conversation about staying—about the daily courage it takes not to bolt when responsibility feels heavier than reward. But there is a moment beyond staying, a moment most men never describe out loud.

It is the stretch of road where the finish line is finally in sight and all the adrenaline that used to push you forward has leaked out through months—sometimes years—of quiet attrition. You are still on your feet. Still moving in the right direction. But if you are honest, you are now propelled less by passion and more by the simple fact that stopping would hurt just as much as continuing.

That is the moment this chapter is written for.

The hand-off.

When the strength that started the journey is no longer enough to complete it, and God slips in beside you—not as a distant coach barking corrections from a sideline, but as the One who intends to cross the tape *with* you, carrying more of the weight than you dare admit.

We all know that completing something significant, whether it's raising children, leading a congregation, maintaining a marriage, caring for aging parents, or staying true to our values, is not an easy task. Beginnings are chaotic and endings are burdensome.

And it is dangerously easy for men to confuse perseverance with self-reliance.

"Just hold on."
"Dig deeper."
"Real men finish what they start."

I have preached all three slogans. They work on posters. They do not keep a heart alive when the night drags on and the road refuses to flatten. Eventually sloganeering gives way to a quieter, more desperate prayer:

"Lord, I don't know how to keep placing one foot in front of the other. You'll have to do something here."

If you are somewhere between that slogan and that prayer, this chapter is for you.

The Last Miles Are Different

Several years ago I agreed—against better judgment—to run a full marathon with a friend from the Marine Corps. I trained convincingly enough to survive the first eighteen miles. Then the course turned inland, away from the cheering crowds that had lined the oceanfront. The road narrowed, the sun climbed, and the once-delightful idea of finishing degenerated into the simple necessity of not collapsing.

Something strange happened at mile twenty. My friend, who had glided through the earlier miles like a gazelle, began to slow. Meanwhile, another runner—a gray-haired man at least two decades our senior—seemed to float past both of us. He didn't look dramatic. He didn't look angry. He just looked… steady.

Later, after I crawled across the finish line and promised God, my wife, and my hamstrings I would never repeat the experiment, I found the gray-haired marvel at the recovery tent. He handed me a cup of lukewarm sports drink and said, almost casually, "You learn the race changes after mile twenty. The real finish starts there. Everything before that is just waking your legs up."

That sentence has stayed with me, usually not in reference to running shoes but to marriage, ministry, parenting, recovery, grief, and the long obedience of discipleship.

The final stretch is qualitatively different.

It does not ask for louder enthusiasm.
It asks for a different source of strength.

Paul understood that shift. Near the end of his life, writing from a Roman prison cell, he did not boast, "I sprinted the whole way." He wrote, "I have fought the good fight, I have finished the race, I have kept the faith." That is not triumphant hype. That is scarred truth. Earlier in that same letter he admitted something most men avoid saying: "The Lord stood with me and strengthened me."

Paul was describing the hand-off.

He did not finish because he was a spiritual superhero. He finished because God stepped close enough to make finishing possible.

When Grit Gives Out

Grit is a gift. It builds muscles of discipline. It teaches you to show up. It keeps you from quitting too early.

But grit was never designed to bear eternal weight.

It is a human resource, and therefore it is exhaustible. If you live long enough—or lead anything meaningful long enough—you will reach a moment that drains the last spoonful of grit from the drawer. And the cruel part is this: it often happens near the end, when you thought you were supposed to be strongest.

A business founder I know reached that moment during a global supply chain collapse that threatened to erase twenty years of work overnight. He described the experience over coffee, voice flat with fatigue: "I kept telling myself, 'I've solved problems before. I can solve this.' Then one night I sat alone in the warehouse staring at unpaid orders and realized I had no more tricks."

Then he said, quietly, "I finally prayed—not the eloquent kind. Just a gasp: 'God, if you don't carry this, it dies.'"

The company survived. But he told me the survival was not the miracle. The miracle was what happened inside him when he finally stopped worshipping competence. He discovered something that looks like weakness but is actually spiritual maturity: the ability to say, *I cannot finish this with me.*

That is not failure. That is graduation.

A pastor I know buried three congregants in one month and could not preach without his throat tightening. A father I love watched a child spiral into addiction and realized his control was an illusion. A leader who had always been the encourager woke up one morning unable to generate a single motivational sentence.

These men did not lack character. They reached terrain grit was never built to cross.

What feels like collapse is often the invitation to discover the strength that finishes.

A Marathon I Didn't Finish Alone

Let me tell you one more running story, because God used it to embarrass and educate me at the same time.

A year after that marathon, against earlier vows, I signed up again. I told myself the second attempt would be about redemption, but secretly it was about proving something. I wanted a better time. A cleaner finish. A little glory.

Two weeks before race day, a nasty head cold shredded my breathing. I should have deferred. But male stubbornness is a predictable disease, and I toed the start line full of nasal decongestant and bravado.

Predictably, my lungs quit early. By mile ten, every breath felt like inhaling through a straw. At mile sixteen, I began weaving. That is when a volunteer medic stepped onto the course, put an arm around my waist, and half-dragged, half-escorted me to a medical station.

"You're done," he said.

I protested through snot and ego. He didn't negotiate. He handed me a thermal blanket, forced fluids down my throat, and called my wife—whose face communicated relief and a lecture still in draft form.

I did not finish that marathon.

Yet something holy lingered in the way I was carried off the course. It dismantled the illusion that finishing is the only noble outcome. Sometimes the noble outcome is being wise enough—or sick enough—to let somebody stronger intervene.

Looking back, I see how the Holy Spirit has done that across my adult life. When I sway toward collapse, He intervenes, often through the arms of a brother who refuses to let me pretend I'm fine. Accepting help does not feel heroic. It feels humiliating.

Only later do I realize how close I came to deeper injury.

So if the end of your race requires more help than you planned, do not assume you failed. You may be living the most honest paragraph of your life.

Biblical Portraits of a Finish Carried by God

Consider Moses.

After decades of leading people who complained about water, food, leadership, and each other, God led him up a mountain where he could see the Promised Land—but not cross into it. To modern eyes, that feels like a tragic anti-climax. Yet Scripture says Moses' strength had not evaporated. His finish line was not geographic; it was relational. God Himself buried him. The end, it turns out, was not "arrival." It was being escorted home by the One who carried Israel through the wilderness.

Or look at Elijah.

The prophet who called down fire also collapsed under a broom tree, begging God to take his life. God did not scold him. He fed him. Let him sleep. Fed him again. Then recommissioned him. Elijah's story is God's refusal to equate spiritual usefulness with emotional energy.

Paul, as we've said, finished in a cell. Weak in body, strong in Spirit. Rome thought it had contained him. Heaven was dictating immortality through him.

In every story, the thread is not a man who "found more grit."
It is a God who shouldered His servant through the door marked Finish.

The Temptation to Clench Fists at the End

Men cherish the ability to grip.

We grip steering wheels, decisions, schedules, paychecks, children's futures, church budgets, retirement accounts, reputations, outcomes.

Somewhere in the final mile, God asks for open palms.

Not because He enjoys stripping men. But because clenched fists cannot receive. When we refuse to let go, He will sometimes pry finger by finger until what remains is surrender. It feels like loss. It is actually liberation.

A missionary I admire spent three decades planting churches in Southeast Asia. He assumed he'd die there. Then a sudden government shift forced his entire team to leave within forty-eight hours. While packing, he felt anger rise: "I gave my life to this soil, and you let a visa officer end it?"

On the flight home he read words he'd preached for years: "Unless a grain of wheat falls into the ground and dies…" He said it hit him like turbulence. Finishing in that field was his dream, but finishing is God's prerogative.

He now trains younger leaders. The churches are still thriving under local elders. He told me, "I thought finishing meant gripping the plow until my last breath. God thought finishing meant placing it in their hands. Same kingdom—different grip."

Unlearning the Hero Narrative

Every culture crafts a hero narrative: win, conquer, retire with applause.

Kingdom culture tells an upside-down story: yield, serve, sometimes disappear, and be known deeply by God.

If you import society's hero story into discipleship, you will interpret weariness as defeat and obscurity as punishment. But Jesus calls the seed "successful" not when it stays visible, but when it falls and produces fruit.

In my twenties, I wanted ministry to look like a highlight reel.

Now, what moves me most are scenes nobody records:

- the husband who speaks softly when anger would've impressed the room
- the grandmother who tithes faithfully on fixed income
- the young man who deletes an app before it drags him back into lust
- the father who shows up to dinner exhausted but present

These are not cinematic victories. They are the hidden obedience finishers practice when nobody is counting.

Finishing well is less about dramatic moments and more about cumulative dependence.

What Carrying Feels Like Versus Being Carried

There is a tactile difference between shouldering a burden and being carried with it.

One stiffens your spine.
The other melts your knees.

One afternoon my youngest son—five years old at the time—insisted on carrying a sack of garden soil from the car to the backyard. The bag weighed more than he did, but he hugged it with heroic determination. After a dozen wobbling steps, he froze, eyes brimming with frustration.

I bent down, wrapped my arms around both boy and sack, and lifted.

He kept his grip on the soil, but the weight no longer distorted his frame. I felt him relax. His hands still clung, but his body rested.

That moment is the gospel in backyard form.

God does not always confiscate the assignment.
He steps under it.

So if you keep praying for weightlessness and it doesn't come, don't miss the relief He's already offering: strength that accompanies instead of removes.

The proof of being carried is not "everything got easier."
It is this: *you are still moving, and you know it isn't just you.*

Accepting God's Pace

Some finishes arrive sooner than expected—a diagnosis, a layoff, a betrayal, a child leaving early. Other finishes stretch longer than you imagined— prolonged caregiving, delayed breakthroughs, sustained hardship.

In both scenarios, the temptation is to resent the pace.

A friend once spent three days on a silent retreat asking God to reveal the next decade of his life. God gave him one sentence: "Slow is not punishment."

That dismantled him.

So much exhaustion comes not from tasks, but from sprinting under a stopwatch God never set.

Finishing with God's strength means adopting God's pace—usually slower than ambition, faster than apathy. The pace of seedtime and harvest. The pace of Sabbath. The pace of Jesus walking almost everywhere He went… except to a cross He would not delay.

Practicing Release

Finishing well involves deliberate acts of release—transferring responsibility, blessing successors, forgiving old grievances, relinquishing outcomes, even laying down some dreams.

Release is not resignation.
Release is stewardship.

A leader who clings too long can strangle what God wants to grow. A father who micromanages adult children suffocates their adulthood. A man who refuses to face mortality robs others of the witness of hope.

Release often sounds like this prayer:
"Lord, it is Yours. If You return it, I will tend it. If You remove it, I will not claw."

Sometimes the thing returns refined. Sometimes it leaves and bears more fruit in someone else's hands.

I watched a mentor preach his last sermon after forty-two years in one pulpit. He stepped down before scandal, before bitterness, before his body forced it. I asked how he knew.

He smiled: "I started asking God, 'Who is next?' instead of asking, 'How long can I keep going?' When the first question became more thrilling than the second, I had my answer."

He still teaches sometimes. Mostly, he cheers. And I've seen tears in his eyes as younger voices preach old gospel truths. He released the microphone and found the joy of echoes.

Companion

Strength

God's strength often arrives wearing human skin.

When Naomi returned empty, Ruth became God's provision. When Paul suffered, friends "refreshed" him. When Moses tired, Aaron and Hur held his arms.

Finishing alone is not heroic. It is hazardous.

If you don't have companions like that, ask God boldly. Tell Him you need a Jonathan. Then keep your eyes open—God's gifts rarely match our preferred packaging. They match our need.

And when they arrive, don't apologize for leaning. Lean hard.

Forward Motion

Brother, if your legs tremble on this stretch of road, remember the gray-haired runner's smile: the race changes after mile twenty.

God is not disappointed that your stride shortened. He anticipated it. He stationed manna along the route, companions on the shoulder, and Himself beside you.

You do not have to hold on until the end.
God holds you through the end.

Your job is simpler—and harder—than you think: keep handing Him whatever weight slides down your arms. Keep opening fists. Keep telling the truth. Keep receiving.

The strength to finish has never been yours to manufacture.

It is His to supply.

Transition to What Comes Next

In the next chapter we will talk about what heaven calls success—about hearing "Well done," not because you never stumbled, but because you learned to rely.

For now, hear this whispered over your heaving lungs: the God who began this good work in you is the One who will complete it.

Keep walking, friend. You are closer than you think.

And you will not cross the line alone.

Chapter 15 - Well Done Requires Dependence

Lie: *"God rewards output."*

Truth: *God honors faithfulness rooted in reliance.*

The Applause We All Secretly Want

Last night I walked into my boys' room to say goodnight and found plastic trophies lined across the dresser like a miniature Hall of Fame. One was for a thirdgrade spelling bee, one for a neighborhood soccer league, another for "Most Improved" in basketball. My youngest had placed a flashlight behind them so they glowed like gold.

I smiled, kissed their foreheads, whispered a prayer, and clicked the light off—but long after I closed the door, the picture stayed with me.

Because the truth is, we never outgrow the desire for trophies; we just swap plastic for something shinier.

Wins at work. Respect from peers. Numbers on a spreadsheet. Retweets and mentions. A bigger house, a nicer truck, a fuller calendar where somebody always needs us.

Men learn early that life applauds output, so we push to produce it. And somewhere in the push we start confusing the scoreboard with the story God is writing.

Chapter 14 reminded us that finishing well means leaning on God's grip, not ours. But finishing well is different from hearing, **"Well done."**

One is endurance; the other is evaluation. One is how you get to the end; the other is what the Owner of the vineyard says when you hand over the harvest.

So tonight, as those plastic trophies still glimmer in my mind, I want to ask a harder question:

When God measures a life—what does He weigh?

I used to assume He weighed results. Sermons preached. Projects completed. People helped. Churches planted. Kids raised. Bills paid. Boxes checked. If the pile was high enough, heaven's doors opened like the standing ovation after a victory lap.

But years of ministry—and the exhaustion that came with those years— forced me to read Scripture slower. When I did, I realized something both liberating and unsettling:

God has never been impressed by output. He is looking for dependence.

The Man Who Carried Everything

Let me introduce you to Jacob—not the patriarch, but a man who sat across from me at a diner two years ago.

Jacob is sixfootthree, runs triathlons for fun, and built a tech company that sold for seven figures before his thirtyfifth birthday. He loves Jesus, sponsors missionaries, mentors students, and teaches a smallgroup Bible study every Wednesday night.

In other words, Jacob owns every trophy the modern Christian scoreboard offers.

But that day, his hands trembled so badly he had to grip the coffee mug with both palms. He hadn't slept more than three hours a night in months. His wife had gently suggested counseling; his doctor was checking blood pressure twice a week.

"I don't know what's wrong with me," he whispered. "I'm doing everything right, and I still feel like I'm drowning."

I asked him what the word *success* meant.

He stared at the ceiling as if the definition might be tiled there. Then he said, quietly:

"Showing up for everyone who's counting on me."

No wonder he was drowning.

The list of "everyone" never ends. Investors count on him. Employees count on him. Volunteers count on him. Missionaries, students, family, friends, wife, kids—countless eyes look to Jacob for provision or direction. And every set of eyes feels like proof he is worth something only so long as he never drops the ball.

I opened to Matthew 25—the parable of the talents. Jacob knew it by heart. But this time we slowed down.

"Tell me," I said, "what's the first compliment the master gives?"

Jacob answered automatically: "Good and faithful."

I nodded. "Is either word about production?"

He frowned. Faithful, yes. Good, maybe. But doubling the talents felt like the real point.

So we traced the theme across Scripture—places where God's commendation shows up, places where "reward" gets defined.

Over and over, the pattern emerged:

God does not applaud capacity. He applauds faithfulness— which is just surrender in motion.

Jacob stared into his empty coffee cup, then whispered:

"So all this weight I've been carrying might not even be on the test?"

Exactly.

Why God Refuses to Grade Your Checklist

If you grew up in church, you probably memorized Ephesians 2:8–9 early on: "For by grace are ye saved through faith… not of works, lest any man should boast."

But most of us treat salvation as the freebie and everything afterward as extra credit. We imagine grace enrolls us in the academy, then we hustle to graduate with honors.

We pile distinction onto the transcript—quiet time streaks, tithing records, marriage seminars, gym routines, volunteer hours, disciplined kids in polished shoes lined up for family photos on Easter Sunday.

Please don't mishear me. God is not against fruitfulness. The Father is not allergic to excellence.

The issue is when the fruit becomes proof of selfsufficiency instead of evidence of abiding.

In John 15 Jesus says, "Herein is my Father glorified, that ye bear much fruit."

But the key line comes earlier:

"He that abideth in me, and I in him, the same bringeth forth much fruit."

The emphasis is connection, not statistics.

A detached branch can't produce apples. It can only pose for pictures.

So God refuses to grade your checklist, because if He did, He would have to reward autonomy. And autonomy is exactly what killed Eden.

The moment Adam and Eve decided they could evaluate good and evil without dependence, they lost communion.

God will never celebrate in you what sin destroyed in them.

A Different Kind of Résumé

Several years ago I attended the funeral of a smalltown pastor named Marvin.

He never spoke to more than two hundred people at once. Never published a book. Never sat on a conference stage. He served the same congregation for fortytwo years—preached, visited widows, baptized infants who later became deacons, sat with families in hospital rooms nobody posts about.

At his graveside, his daughter unfolded a lined notebook she'd found in Marvin's desk. It listed every person he'd prayed for daily since 1983.

There were over a thousand names.

Mine was on page twelve, though he and I had met only twice.

As I watched the casket lower, I realized Marvin's life would look unimpressive on LinkedIn, but heaven's résumé for him must be thick with God's handwriting.

He had been faithful—in obscurity, in sickness, in seasons of zero numerical growth. He stayed where God put him, listened when God spoke, repented when he sinned, loved the people in front of him, and trusted Christ to do the multiplying.

The branch never cut itself from the vine. Jesus says that is success.

What Dependence Looks Like on Tuesday Morning

By now you may be asking, "If God's metric is dependence, how do I know I'm living that way?"

The answer is rhythm, not heroics.

Depending on God feels less like a fireworks finale and more like breathing—quiet, consistent, necessary.

Here's an embarrassing example.

Last year I stepped into a new leadership role at church. Everyone congratulated me, but inside I felt like a kid wearing his dad's suit. The first month I worked fifteenhour days, skipped lunch, ignored my wife's gentle reminders to rest. Attendance went up; budgets balanced. I basked in silent pride.

Then my oldest son's birthday arrived.

I stood in the kitchen, fumbling to cut a crooked slice of cake, and overheard him tell his friend:

"Dad's busy a lot, but one day when he's not, we'll play basketball again."

I carried that sentence into prayer the next morning.

"Lord, look how much is happening—people are joining small groups, the building loan got paid down, our webcast reached fifteen countries."

I was showing God the trophies. He was listening to an elevenyearold boy who missed his father.

I heard a whisper I couldn't dismiss:

"I didn't ask you to neglect the boy I gave you to impress people I didn't give you."

That day I deleted half my calendar. Our staff now jokes that my favorite sentence is, "No is a complete answer."

We haven't lost momentum; in some ways we've gained it, because I'm not piloting from exhaustion anymore.

That is what practical dependence feels like:

- Work from rest.
- Lead from listening.
- Measure success by obedience to the next thing God actually said— not the endless things people expect.

When Dependence Feels Like Failure

Dependence is beautiful in theory and brutal in execution, because it often requires saying "yes" to something lesser in the world's eyes or saying "no" to something shinier.

You might walk away from a promotion that doubles your salary but triples your travel days. You might stay in a marriage the world calls hopeless because God whispered, "My grace is sufficient here." You might give sacrificially when saving would seem wiser. You might keep pastoring thirty people in a rented gym while your friend opens a megachurch across town.

And the moment you obey, insecurity flares:

What if I'm wasting potential? What if this is laziness disguised as spiritual conviction? What if ten years from now I regret not chasing bigger?

Those questions assume a scoreboard of output.

God's scoreboard is simpler:

Were you where I asked you to be? Did you rely on Me to bear fruit—even if it stayed invisible for a while?

Consider Jesus on the cross. From a worldly perspective, His ministry ended in failure—abandoned, humiliated, crucified like a criminal.

Yet in that apparent defeat He accomplished the most fruitful act in history.

How?

By unwavering dependence: "Father, into Thy hands I commend My spirit."

If the Savior tied success to surrender, how bold are we to tie ours to metrics?

The Weight You're Not Built to Carry

Here's the truth men hate and need:

Output is never fully in your control. Faithfulness always is.

Noah preached for decades and convinced almost nobody. Hebrews still calls him faithful. Ezekiel was told upfront his audience would not listen. His obedience still mattered. John the Baptist had one core message and one short life, and Jesus called him the greatest born among women.

When I sit with men near burnout, most of their anxiety comes from outcomes they can't guarantee:

- Will the merger close?
- Will my teenager choose Christ?
- Will my parents' bills bankrupt us?
- Will my marriage recover?
- Will I be enough?

Behind many sleepless nights is a man secretly trying to occupy the throne of universe management.

Dependence unseats that illusion.

It hands the calculator back to God and says:

"Teach me faithfulness in the next ten minutes. The rest is Yours."

Redefining the Master's Words

"Well done, thou good and faithful servant… thou hast been faithful over a few things…"

Few vs. many.

The servant did not obsess over "many." He stewarded the "few."

In modern terms, you may be faithful over:

- a few diapers changed
- a few invoices processed
- a few students loved
- a few emails answered kindly
- a few parents visited
- a few arguments apologized for first

Heaven sees significance in every spoonful of soup slid across a nursinghome table done for Christ's sake.

One day you will stand in line behind saints who never touched a microphone, and you will hear thunderous honor as the King celebrates decades of hidden obedience.

The world missed their names. Heaven did not.

The Freedom of an Audience of One

I once preached at a conference where the speaker before me received a standing ovation that felt like an avalanche. I stepped up, delivered what I thought was solid, then returned to my seat to polite applause.

For the next two hours I replayed every sentence, comparing myself to the man who brought the house down.

My friend leaned over, saw the frustration, and said six words that rescued me:

"Only one seat really matters."

The fear of man links success to applause. The fear of the Lord ties success to obedience.

One hardens you into fragile ego. The other softens you into confident dependence.

Dependence and Reward

Dependence doesn't eliminate reward; it purifies motive.

You can't earn inheritance, but you can steward it. The Father trains you in dependence so you can handle kingdom resources without pretending you generated them.

And here's the twist: even the rewards loop back into dependence.

Revelation describes crowns—real honor, real glory—and then it shows the redeemed casting those crowns at Jesus' feet.

Even in eternity, trophies don't stay on the dresser. They go back to the rightful Owner.

How to Practice Hearing "Well Done" Now

The most transformative shift in my daytoday life came when I stopped waiting for the final evaluation and started inviting it nightly.

Before sleep, I ask two questions:

"Lord, where did I walk in step with Your Spirit today?" "And where did I take the wheel back?"

No selfflagellation. No performance review panic. Just a Father and a son reviewing film together.

Sometimes the highlight reel is embarrassingly short. Other nights I'm stunned by what He counts as success:

- a patient reply to a rude email
- five unhurried minutes listening to my teenager
- a whispered prayer for a stranger at the gas pump
- an apology offered quickly instead of defended stubbornly

Dependence sharpens your awareness of these moments because they are exactly the ones you would overlook chasing "bigger" achievements.

Over time, this practice rewires you.

You notice prompts faster. Release control sooner. Repent quicker. Sleep deeper.

Not because you did everything— but because you did the next thing with
Him.

A Word for the Overachiever

You may worry this chapter will dull your edge. You have quotas, deadlines,
shareholders, responsibilities that don't care about your theology.

Dependence doesn't cancel responsibility. It aligns it.

Joseph still managed grain. Daniel still served in government. Lydia still ran
a business.

But their identity didn't hang from outcomes like a noose.

When dependence drives you, excellence becomes worship instead of
selfworth.

You work hard, but results don't own you.

If sales dip, your value remains fixed. If the launch flops, your son still
wants you in the driveway. If the board applauds, you send the praise
upward instead of hoarding it.

Dependence turns performance into offering.

A Final Story Before We Turn the Page

When I was twelve, my dad asked me to help paint the backyard fence. He
handed me a small brush, showed me the strokes, and left to paint the larger
side.

I attacked my section with zeal and terrible technique. By noon it looked
like modern art. Drips everywhere. Bare wood showing. I panicked, grabbed
more paint, and smeared harder. The mess grew.

Dad walked over, saw the disaster, and smiled.

"Let's finish together," he said.

He took my hand and guided each stroke. Two hours later the section looked flawless. That evening Mom praised the fence, and Dad said, "He did great, didn't he?"

My cheeks burned because I knew who had truly done the work.

But Dad wasn't lying.

He wasn't rewarding my performance. He was commending my willingness to let him take over.

Someday we will stand before the Judge who is also Abba Father. He will point to the life behind us and say, **"Well done."**

And we will know—perhaps more clearly than ever—that every straight line was His steadying hand over ours. Every smooth coat was His skill through our surrendered fingers. Every beautiful result was grace, compounded by grace, signed with grace.

The sentence itself will be final proof:

Success was never about output. It was always about Who held the brush.

Transition to the Finish Line

In the final chapter we will look back across the distance we've traveled together. Not to flex spiritual muscles or count planks of fence, but to trace the hand of the One who steadied us when ours shook.

Until then, rest here:

The applause of heaven hinges not on how much you carried, but on whether you let the Father carry you.

And that is a verdict you can start living under right now—long before the last nail is tapped, long before the final breath.

Because **"Well done" is simply dependence, spoken with joy.**

Chapter 16 - Still Standing Because God Sustained Me

Lie: *"I'm still here because I was strong enough."*

Truth: *You're still here because God was faithful.*

The Quiet Surprise of Survival

Pause with me for a moment and notice something that rarely gets our attention:

You are still here.

The deadlines you thought would break you have come and gone. The grief you were certain would swallow you whole has not had the last word. The mistakes you swore would ruin your life have not written your final chapter.

You have lines on your face you did not have ten years ago, scars on your soul you never asked for, and memories both bitter and bright — but you are still here, walking, breathing, believing.

We are so accustomed to measuring our lives by what is next that we seldom linger long enough to marvel at what God has already carried us through. Survival feels ordinary because it has become our normal. But if we could step outside our own timeline for even a minute and view it the way heaven does, we would be stunned.

The enemy predicted your collapse. Your anxiety rehearsed it. Your critics expected it. Even you, some nights, assumed tomorrow would be too heavy.

Yet here you are — still married, still leading, still opening Scripture, still returning to God's presence with all the honesty you can gather.

You may not feel impressive, but the fact that you are standing is evidence of something deeper than willpower.

Scripture calls it **preservation**. Grace calls it **enough**. Jesus calls it this: **"No one can pluck them out of My Father's hand."**

If everything you have read in this book could be condensed into a single sentence, it might be this:

The power that sustains you is not inside you but underneath you — and it has never once considered letting you slip.

Remembering What Carried Us

When the Israelites crossed the Jordan and stepped into the Promised Land, God told them to collect twelve stones and build a memorial.

The instruction felt strange. Why pause to stack rocks when an entire country still had to be conquered?

Because God understood how quickly people forget what carried them.

Victory has a way of editing its own story.

Two years after the miracle, the memory sounds like: **We made it.**

A decade later it becomes: **I always believed we could.**

An entire generation later it's reduced to folklore: **Did that really happen?**

So God broke the cycle. He asked them to memorialize the moment. The stones did not make them holy; they made them honest.

Each time a future son asked his father, "What do these stones mean?" the story would roll off his tongue:

We were powerless against that river. God opened it, and His strength carried us across on dry ground.

You and I need memorials too.

Not marble statues or plaques, but places in our memory where we freezeframe God's interventions long enough that the credit cannot drift subtly toward ourselves.

We need to retell the days we almost quit, the nights we could not sleep, the medical report that sounded like a period but turned out to be a comma, the season we lived off prayers whispered through clenched teeth.

Because if we do not remember, we will rewrite. And if we rewrite, we will inevitably promote ourselves to a role we never actually played.

My Own Pile of Stones

Let me lay my stones in front of you as honestly as I can.

I spent my late twenties convinced I could outrun limitation. Ministry opportunities kept growing, travel picked up, and invitations stacked faster than sleep. I saw every open door as confirmation that God wanted me inside it. Declining felt like disbelief, so I said yes — always, immediately, without discernment.

I preached about grace during the day and ran on caffeine and adrenaline at night, assuming that pace was faithfulness.

Eventually my body pushed back.

One afternoon, halfway through a teaching session, my peripheral vision collapsed into gray static and I felt the ground shift. I gripped the lectern harder, forced my way through the final minutes, smiled at the closing prayer, and practically crawled to the greenroom.

A doctor later called it **stressinduced near syncope**. My wife called it **unsustainable**. God called it **mercy**.

I wish I could tell you I slowed down immediately. I did not.

But cracks kept appearing — short temper, shallow prayer, persistent fatigue I justified as "being poured out for the gospel."

The crash finally came in the form of a voice I trusted: my mentor. He looked me in the eye and did not congratulate my productivity. He told me I was bleeding slowly and everyone could see it but me.

Then he said a sentence that lodged beneath my ribs:

"Son, God is not proud of you for killing yourself."

That conversation became my memorial. Not because it felt good — it hurt — but because it forced me to face the lie that stamina equals spirituality.

I began canceling engagements, seeing a counselor, taking real rest days, and relearning how to pray without rehearsing my résumé to God.

Five years have passed. The opportunities are still there, but my answers often sound like discernment now, not desperation. I have margin to hear my children laugh at dinner. I have capacity to listen when my wife says she is tired. And the pulpit, ironically, feels lighter because I no longer stand in it pretending I can carry the weight alone.

If someone asks why I am still standing, the answer is embarrassingly simple:

God sustained me — through correction, through community, through the mercy of limits I once resented.

My survival is a miracle wearing ordinary clothes.

The Illusion of SelfPreservation

Men like us rarely talk about preservation. We talk about optimization.

We buy running shoes with carbon plates, read articles on highintensity interval training, track macros and screen time and step counts. Stewardship is wise; obsession is idolatry in a lab coat.

During one leadership retreat, an executive proudly shared his routine: four hours of sleep, two protein shakes, morning emails at 4:30 a.m., a midday treadmill desk session, and evening strategy calls with AsiaPacific clients.

He expected applause.

The room gave him admiration — and silent pity.

His calendar looked bulletproof, but his soul looked starved.

Selfpreservation is a fragile god. The moment you slacken the reins, it punishes you with panic.

True preservation — the kind that does not fray at the edges — has never been entrusted to human hands.

David recognized that when he wrote:

"The LORD is my shepherd; I shall not want."

Notice the tense: *is*. Not *was*. Not *will be if I earn it*.

Present. Perpetual. Never outsourced.

God does not merely repair us; He keeps us. Not like a machine kept in a garage, but like a child held in a father's arms.

Underneath are the everlasting arms.

The world calls that sentimental. The kingdom calls it structural.

The Gift of Scars

Look at your own life's landscape. You will see peaks where God's power felt obvious — opportunities you didn't apply for, provisions you didn't predict, flights that landed safely after gripping turbulence.

But do not overlook the valleys. They are memorials too, carved with a steadier hand than mountaintops.

I think of the night our youngest was admitted to the pediatric ICU with a respiratory virus. Machines hummed, alarms chimed, my wife's eyes looked equal parts fierce and frightened. I stood unable to fix anything.

So I did what felt embarrassingly passive: I prayed. Not with eloquence, but with the next breath. And the next. And the next.

Twentyfour hours later her oxygen stabilized, and three days later we carried her out of the hospital, smaller than before but very much alive.

When I relay that story now, I do not glorify the power of prayer in abstract terms. I glorify the One who sustained my daughter's lungs when medicine reached its limit.

The doctor's skill was real; God's breath was deeper.

The scar remains — the memory of pacing cold linoleum floors — but it testifies louder than any unbroken streak of health could.

Jesus kept His scars after resurrection. They were not cosmetic oversights. They were evidence — proof that death had tried and failed.

Your scars tell a similar story: **weakness tried, but grace prevailed.**

Turning Gratitude into Posture

Grateful reflection can remain a feeling or mature into posture.

Feelings visit; posture abides.

Posture kneels in the morning not because the day is heavy yet, but because it will be. Posture thanks God for coffee and continuity, for the chance to try again, for the ordinary miracle of a stillbeating heart. Posture refuses to clock out of dependence after the crisis subsides.

Paul modeled it:

"Having obtained help of God, I continue unto this day."

Obtained — past tense. Continue — present tense.

One flows into the other like river into sea. The help didn't expire; it evolved into daily fuel.

Early in my marriage, I thanked my wife with flowers the day after her birthday and assumed the gesture bought me credit for a while. She appreciated it — but wise spouses know: gratitude hoarded eventually sours.

Gratitude expressed becomes culture.

The same is true with God. Occasional thanks is polite. Continuous thanks is alignment.

It keeps the soul facetoface with the Source instead of flirting with selfcredit.

Why You're Still Here

Let me address the quiet suspicion some of you feel reading this final chapter.

You survived — but barely.

Your marriage bears hairline fractures. Your savings account looks thin. Your prayer life is more sighs than sentences. You wonder if calling this "God's sustaining power" is spiritual exaggeration.

Brother, the fact that decay has not swallowed you is not exaggeration.

You may limp, but you limp forward. You may doubt, but you doubt inside covenant.

Like Jacob after wrestling the angel, you walk differently now. The limp is not defeat; it is demonstration that God allowed you to wrestle and did not let you perish in the process.

You are here because sovereign hands said, **Enough. He will not fall beyond this point.**

Sometimes those hands shielded you from crisis. Sometimes they shielded you inside crisis. Sometimes they let you feel the full quake so you would remember what unshakeable means.

But always, they held.

I have watched friends bury their parents and still bless the Lord. I have watched leaders lose positions and still serve quietly in unseen places. I have watched men walk through rehab, through bankruptcy, through betrayal, and come out without the scent of bitterness.

None of them credit resilience. They credit Presence.

Finishing Without the Pose

Culture loves a victory pose: fists raised, chest out, fireworks.

But finishing well in the kingdom rarely looks photoready. More often it's a man on his knees whispering, **"Thank You for carrying me."**

I officiated a funeral for a grandfather who lived modestly, loved ferociously, and never owned a social media account. His final weeks were laced with pain, but his final journal entry read:

"Jesus has not failed me yet, and He will not start tonight."

That line — scrawled in shaky penmanship — outpreached my eulogy.

When I imagine my own finish line, I don't fantasize about stadium applause. I picture God's hand beneath my elbow, steadying a frail body, and His voice saying,

"You never realized how much I was carrying you, did you?"

And I think I will weep — not from regret, but from relief that the illusion of selfsufficiency will finally be impossible to maintain.

Handing the Story Down

One of the tragedies of busy masculinity is that we stay silent about stories that could keep our sons from repeating our mistakes.

We teach them to change a tire, secure a mortgage rate, throw a curveball. But how often do we sit on the edge of their beds and tell them:

"I almost lost myself once, and here is how God rescued me."

If you do not tell them who sustained you, the world will gladly tell them who to credit: hustle, talent, grit.

Those substitutes taste thrilling until they turn bitter.

Give the next generation a better narrative. Let them hear the tremor in your voice when you speak of the night you thought faith folded but heaven held. Let them see the tears you don't often allow because men are supposed to be composed.

Tearless testimony is sanitized. Honest testimony bleeds.

Imagine your grandson one day asking, "Granddad, how did you stay married fifty years?"

And imagine answering, **"Because God bound our hearts when our own resolve unraveled."**

That admission may impart more strength than any pep talk about compatibility ever could.

Living as Sustained Men

So where do we go from here?

We keep going — strangely hopeful, properly dependent, suspicious of any strength that brags.

We plan, but we don't presume. We train, but we don't trust in training. We gather mentors and doctors and counselors because God often sustains through them, yet we trace every line of support back to its first cause: the God who authored breath.

Will we still grow tired? Absolutely. Will we still misjudge capacity? Unfortunately.

But collapse is no longer a crisis of identity; it's an echo reminding us to return to the vine.

I used to fear mornings when I woke up already weary, as if they signaled moral deficiency. Now I receive them as an early nudge toward the fountain.

Weariness is not treason; it is the body requesting fresh manna.

The old manna was never meant to carry into today.

An Invitation, Not a SendOff

As we close this chapter — and with it, this book — I don't picture you shutting the cover with a surge of selfconfidence.

I picture you exhaling. Maybe even loosening the shoulders you didn't realize were knotted. And hearing a still, small voice say:

We can keep walking together.

God is not congratulating you for finishing a reading plan. He is inviting you deeper into the reality these pages pointed toward.

The classroom portion is over; the fieldwork continues.

And in that field, strength will still run out, sometimes faster than you expect.

The difference now is that you won't misinterpret depletion as failure. You'll recognize it as the opening through which power flows.

A Final Prayer of Gratitude

Father, Thank You for every man who has made it this far — not just through ink and paper, but through nights of confusion, days of pressure, years of responsibility that outweighed his own strength. Thank You that he is still breathing, still reaching, still willing to learn what dependence means. Remind him where the credit belongs. Repair the places where shame still whispers that he should have been stronger. Reenchant his memory with moments You intervened, so he cannot retell the story without mentioning Your name. Teach him to build memorials — conversations, journal entries, bedtime stories, prayers whispered over the steering wheel — so that when the next storm comes, gratitude will already be a wellworn path. And when he finally crosses his finish line, let his last conscious act on this earth be surrender into the arms that have been carrying him all along. In Jesus' name — who sustains, who keeps, who finishes what He starts — Amen.

Still standing — because God was faithful.

Closing Reflection

We have walked together through the uncomfortable truth that your limits are not proof of failure—they are the fingerprints of design. From Eden's borrowed breath to Paul's borrowed strength, every page has circled the same confession: **a man was never meant to power his own life.** Real strength begins the moment you admit you've reached the end of yours. That is where God, not your grit, steps in—not to scold you, but to carry what you can't.

And we have stared burnout in the face and refused to call it shame. Exhaustion isn't a verdict; it's a dashboard light that says, **"Pull over—let the Mechanic lift the hood."** When you treat fatigue as a signal instead of a sentence, you give God room to do what discipline and caffeine never could.

Then we practiced daily dependence—quiet rhythms of prayer, honest surrender, tiny acts of obedience that look ordinary until you notice how much lighter you're walking. Grace stopped being an emergency exit and became the oxygen in your lungs. Weakness, once an enemy, became a doorway—one God walks through without confusing His power with your image.

Finishing well, we discovered, is not clutching the steering wheel until your knuckles bleed. It is resting in a grip that has never slipped. God carries what you were never built to survive holding, and He is strong enough for both of you.

So here we are at the edge of the last page—but not the end of the invitation. Tomorrow the alarm will ring, responsibilities will line up, and the old lie of self-reliance will clear its throat. When it does, remember this journey. Whisper, **"Lord, I don't have to be enough today because You already are."**

Step out in borrowed strength. Move at the pace of grace. And let the world see a man still standing—not because he never grew weary, but because God never stopped being strong.

Father, keep turning us back toward You—quickly, humbly, daily.
Teach us to live with open hands and quiet trust.
And when we're tired, remind us: we are not alone. Amen.

Acknowledgements

I would like to begin by expressing my excitement about the privilege of writing this book—not simply because my name appears on the cover, but because I know I will return to these pages myself to relearn the lessons I still need. Although I held the pen, I cannot claim sole credit for its creation. God wrote this book through me, and I am deeply grateful that He entrusted me with the gift and responsibility of bringing it into the world.

The funny thing about asking God for help is that you never quite know how, when, or through whom that help will arrive. For me, God has always revealed His vision through the very things He placed in my heart—my passions, my reflections, and especially my writing. This project became one of the ways He continued shaping me.

This journey has been emotional, stretching, and deeply transformative. God has been building—and at times rebuilding—me from who I thought I was and who I imagined I wanted to be into the man He already saw in me. I know I have not always been the easiest student, and so I am profoundly grateful for His patience. I lean on Him because He has never failed me.

I believe God was preparing, positioning, and maturing me so that when the moment finally arrived, I would be ready—spiritually, emotionally, and personally—to write this book with clarity and conviction.

I am grateful to everyone who offered thoughtful, honest, and encouraging feedback on one or more chapters, and to all who welcomed me into their lives and relationships. Your openness and trust helped shape the heart of this work.

To my sisters, Dorothy McJoy and Earline Ivybott, and to my brothers, Joe and Tommy Groves—thank you. I don't say it nearly enough, but you are pillars of strength in my life. I have watched you, sometimes from a distance, and I have learned so much from each of you. I am truly thankful.

To my children—John II, Jabari, NJeri, Janai, Kamau, and Jordan—you inspire me every single day. When I look at you, I am reminded of what I am working for. You keep me grounded in the present while motivating me to build a future worthy of you. Your resilience amazes me, and I hope to make you proud and serve as a model of perseverance, purpose, and faith.

Finally, I saved the best for last. To my wife, Serwa Kenyatta Groves (Keni)—thank you for your patience, your support, and your unwavering partnership throughout this process. Thank you for enduring my long hours in the home office and for helping me shape these ideas into something meaningful. Writing this book has been a joy, but reading and reflecting on it has helped me become a better husband and a better man—one God continues to pour into. I am grateful for the gift of you, the woman God placed in my life.

I've been told that this book will help me see you more clearly—your wants, needs, and desires—and guide me in loving you the way you deserve to be loved. Thank you, sincerely, for being my "Helpmeet."

I know I don't always express my feelings aloud, but I want you to know that you are the center of my world. I could not have written this book or pursued any of my goals without your presence, your strength, and your love. You are my Muse, and I finally understand that truth.

www.ingramcontent.com/pod-product-compliance
Lightning Source LLC
Chambersburg PA
CBHW051413050726
47595CB00010B/4041